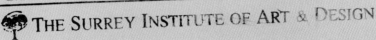
brochure design forum

3

P·I·E Books.

An International Collection of Brochures, Pamphlets and Catalogues

BROCHURE DESIGN FORUM 3
An International Collection of Brochures, Pamphlets and Catalogues

BROCHURE DESIGN FORUM 3
Copyright ©1997 by P·I·E BOOKS

First published in Japan 1997 by: P·I·E BOOKS
#301, 4-14-6 Komagome, Toshima-ku, Tokyo 170, Japan
TEL: 03-3949-5010 FAX: 03-3949-5650

ISBN4-89444-034-2 C3070   324784

Printed in Singapore

Content

はじめに

本書「ブローシュア デザイン フォーラム３」はアメリカをはじめヨーロッパ、アジア、オセアニアなど、世界中から集められたカタログやパンフレット、約200点を業種別に分類しご紹介しております。

　こうしてたくさんの国の作品を一堂に集めてみますと、素材や色の選び方、また構成の仕方やそれぞれのページに散りばめられているアイディアなどに、１人１人のデザイナーの個性を感じると共に、様々な国事情をも感じさせられます。

　今回はコンピューターネットワークや自費出版、またテクノークラブ文化などが雑誌等のメディアで何かと話題のオランダやその周辺諸国からの作品も多く掲載することができました。洋服でレンガを吊り丈夫さをアピールしているアパレルメーカーのカタログや、カラーコピーを使ってわざと荒れた感じを活かしているデザイナーの作品集など・・・これらの国々の作品は、既存の発想とは違うアイディアが感じられ、今後の展開がますます楽しみです。

　小社では、このように広く世界のデザインの状況を捉えていき、皆様の貴重な資料として活用頂けたら幸いに思います。

　最後に、本書制作に当たりまして、すばらしい作品をお送り下さいました皆様に、心より感謝申し上げます。

Foreword

Brochure Design Forum 3 offers a collection of some 200 samples of catalogues and pamphlets originating from America, Europe, Asia and Oceania, and classified according to the type of business they represent.

Assemble artwork from such a large number of different sources, and the overall design concepts and ideas for individual pages, the choice of materials and colors, not only give us a sense of each designer's style but tell us something of the countries they come from as well.

This edition features many brochures from northern Europe including the Netherlands, where computer networking, self-financed publishing and techno music are hot topics in the print media. In one apparel maker's catalogue, pants are used to hoist bricks to demonstrate the toughness of the fabric. Elsewhere, the slightly rough result created by a color copier is used to good effect. The artwork from these countries abounds with unconventional ideas and leaves us wondering what to expect next.

We at PIE Books hope you will find this volume useful as a reference source of graphic design as currently practised in many different parts of the world. We would like to take this opportunity to thank all those who have kindly contributed their artwork for this collection.

Editorial Notes

Credit Format

Client's business and purpose of artwork
クライアントの業種／作品の使用目的

Country where client based / country where artwork produced (if different)
クライアント国名／作品製作国名（同一の場合は1つに省略致しました。）

Year of completion　年度
CD : Creative director
AD : Art director
D : Designer
P : Photographer
I : Illustrator
CW : Copywriter
DF : Design firm
CL : Client
Size (h×w) : サイズ（タテ×ヨコ）

The jacket design uses artwork contributed by Team
One Advertising, Boy Bastiaens, F.D.C. Products Inc.,
Mark Designs, Planet Design Company,
FET Co., Ltd., Signé Lazer & Espai Graphic.

brochure design forum

3

P·I·E Books

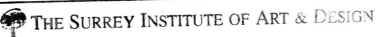

Real Estate   Data & Communications   Paper & Printing   Art & Design   Music & Media   Public & Non-Profit Organizations   Others

1

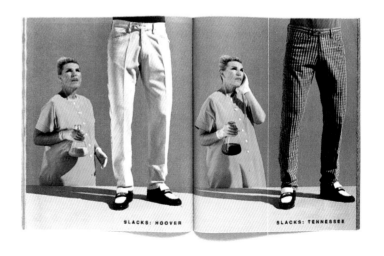

2

アパレルメーカー　製品案内　Apparel Maker　Promotional Brochures　Italy / UK　1996（1）1995（2）
CD, D：Brian Baderman　D：Nick Oates　P：Peter Gehrke　DF：Baderman　CL：Diesel　SIZE：230×295mm

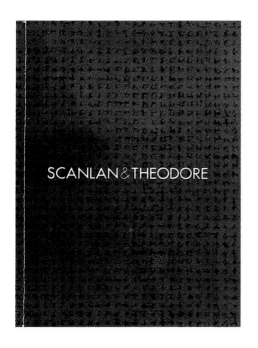

SCANLAN & THEODORE

アパレルメーカー　製品案内
Apparel Maker　Product Brochure
Australia　1996

AD, D : **Fabio Ongarato**

D : **Belle Sambevska**

P : **Michele Aboud**

Stylist : **Alex Zabotto-Bentley**

DF : **Fabio Ongarato Design**

CL : **Scanlan & Theodore**

SIZE : **260 × 185mm**

Spring-Summer
collection 1996

Jacket (RDV-4619)
￥52,000
Pants (RGE-4619)
￥27,000

Knit Running (RGA-1603)
￥72,000
Knit Skirt (RGA-7503)
￥74,000

Jacket (RDV-1620)
￥85,000
Running (RGA-3604)
￥1,900
Skirt (RGC-1620)
￥15,000

Jacket (RDV-4619)
￥54,000
Skirt (RGC-6619)
￥22,000

Jacket (RDV-1617)
￥46,000
Skirt (RGC-2617)
￥15,000

One Piece (RGX-3606)
￥22,000

アパレルメーカー　製品案内
Apparel Maker　Promotional Brochure
Japan / USA　1995

CD, AD : **Richard Seireeni**

D : **Hat Nguyen**

P : **Phillip Dixon**

DF : **Studio Seireeni**

CL : **Jun Co., Ltd.**

SIZE : **340 × 240mm**

アパレルメーカー　製品案内
Apparel Maker　Product Brochure
Brasil　1993

CD, AD : **Sérgio Liuzzi**

CD, AD, D, P : **André de Castro**

DF : **Interface Designers**

CL : **Richards**

SIZE : **170 × 210mm**

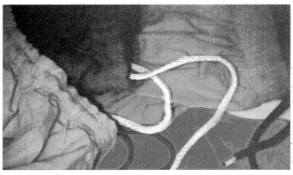

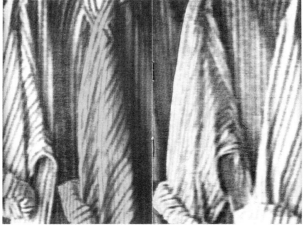

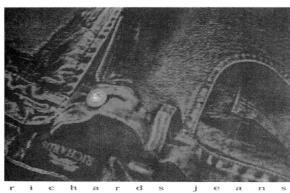

ブティック　商品案内
Fashion Boutique　Product Brochure
Brasil　1994

CD, AD, D : Ruth Klotzel / Paulo Labriola

P : Gui Paganini

CW : Marta Nehring

DF : Estudio Infinito

CL : Claudete e Deca

SIZE : 210 × 140mm

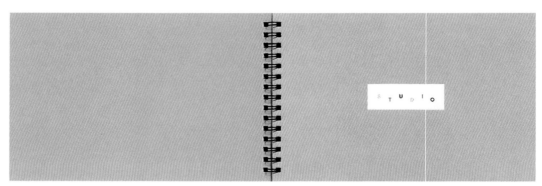

アパレルメーカー　製品案内
Apparel Maker　Promotional Brochure
Hong Kong　1993

CD, AD, D : **Ching Lai Shan**

P : **Kam Ming NG**

DF : **Eye Studio Ltd.**

CL : **Trinity Textiles Ltd.**

SIZE : **140 × 210mm**

JACKET
Wool/Rayon/Cupra
¥39,000

SKIRT
Wool/Rayon/Cupra
¥42,000

PULLOVER
Polyester/Rayon/Wool
¥9,000

POLLOVER

| Off White | Sand Beige | Brown | Black |

JACKET
¥14,000

PULLOVER
¥9,000

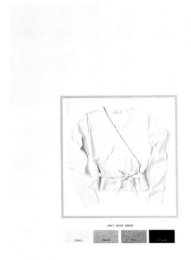

KNIT CACHE-COEUR

| Ivory | Peach | Rose | Black |

KNIT CACHE-COEUR
Rayon/Acrylic
¥16,000

CARDIGAN
Rayon/Acrylic
¥18,000

DRESS
Polyester
¥18,000

SPRING IN COMFORTABLE LIGHT JACKET 4℃ SPRING COLLECTION 199
SPRING 1996
4℃

CAMISOLE
Polyester
¥3,500

JACKET
Wool/Polyester
¥42,000

DRESS
Wool/Polyester
¥29,000

アパレル / アクセサリーメーカー　製品案内
**Apparel / Accessories Maker
Product Brochure**
Japan　1996

AD, DF : **Masuo Kuroda**

P : **Hiroshi Honma /**

Tsutomu Tanaka

CL : **4℃**

SIZE : **297 × 210mm**

テキスタイルメーカー　25周年記念プロモーション　Textile Manufacturer　25th Anniversary Promotional Brochure　Hong Kong　1991

CD. AD · Kan Tai-keung　AD · Freeman Lau Siu Hong　D · Clement Yick Tat Wa　P · C. K. Wong　DF · Kan Tai-keung Design & Associates Ltd.　CL · Kam Lung Textile（Group）Co., Ltd.　SIZE · 295 × 208mm

アパレルメーカー　製品案内　Apparel Maker　Product Brochure　Japan / USA　1994
AD. D : **John Hornall**　D : **Julie Lock / Mary Hermes / Julie Keenan**　DF : **Hornall Anderson Design Works, Inc.**　CW. CL : **Okamoto Corporation**　SIZE : **279×178mm**

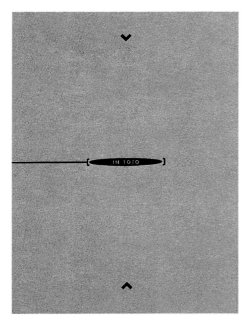

アパレルメーカー　製品案内
Apparel Maker　Product Brochure
USA　1991

CD, AD, D, I, DF : **Planet Design Company**

AD, P, CL : **Dale Stenton**

SIZE : **305 × 221mm**

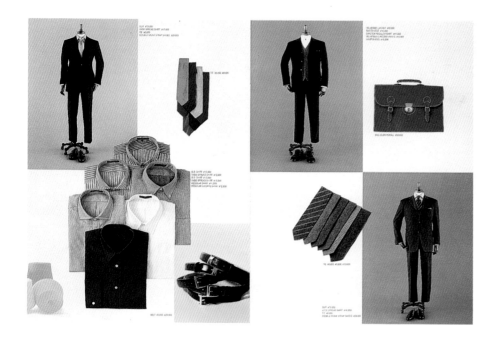

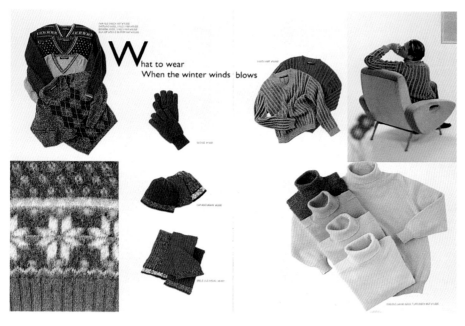

TOMORROWLAND
THE STORE

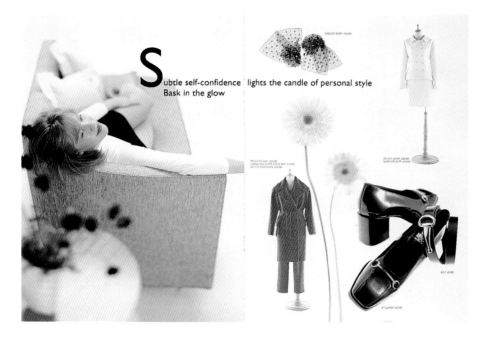

アパレルメーカー　製品案内
Apparel Maker　Product Brochure
Japan　1996

CD : Tamotsu Yagi

P : John Chan / Christiana Ceppas

DF : Tamotsu Yagi Design

CL : Tomorrowland Co., Ltd.

SIZE : 296 × 210mm

アパレルメーカー　製品案内
Apparel Maker　Product Brochure
Japan　1996

CD : Tokuko Maeda

AD. D : Mitsuru Sekino

P : Eddy Kohli

CL : Renown Inc.

SIZE : 363 × 245mm

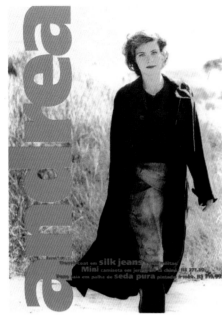

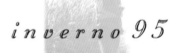

inverno 95

アパレルメーカー　製品案内
Apparel Maker　Product Brochure
Brasil　1995

CD, AD : **Sérgio Liuzzi**

CD, AD, D : **André de Castro**

P : **Nana Moraes**

DF : **Interface Designers**

CL : **Andrea Saletto**

SIZE : **260×180mm**

アパレルメーカー　製品案内
Apparel Maker　Product Catalogue
Japan　1996

CD, AD, D, I : **Mitsuru Sekino**

P : **Shunji Kaida**

CW : **Yasuko Kato**

CL : **Renown Inc.**

SIZE : **297 × 219mm**

アパレルメーカー　製品案内
Apparel Maker　Product Brochure
Japan　1996

CD, AD, D : **Mitsuru Sekino**

P : **Tenjun Kamoshita**

CL : **Renown Inc.**

SIZE : **220 × 110mm**

Hey so what's the rumpus?
We're back, it's almost Spring,
and we're totally ready for it. We're
streamlined, superfied, purified,
relaxed, electrified, plugged into the
beat mindset to start our bodies
swinging, flying, lying, exploring
touring, flaunting, moping, hoping,
painting, entancing, fantasizing-
laxy and crazy we're Spring and
Summer together. X-girls=women
curves up and down colors red,
black, and skyhigh blue, T-shirts
with 3/4 length sleeves and tank
tops too. The skirts are in three
lengths because we couldn't choose. The
dress makes us feel like Anna Karina
a girl living in a woman's body in the
existential landscape of rules
we didn't make. "I'm ready for my
close-up Mr. Godard".
The jeans are crazy, sleek,
straight, tight, flirty and fit,
they stretch and bend or come in
regular all cotton thread.
Oh, yeah, we almost forgot to
tell you, we've thrown out the
sizing-xs,s,m,l,xl, We're now
0,1,2,3,4- it's like new math.
Well ALRIGHT
Let's go NOW!
Daisy ♡ xo ♡ KiM

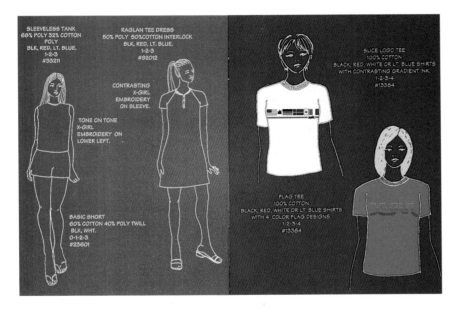

アパレルメーカー　製品案内
Apparel Maker　Product Catalogue
USA　1995

P : **Cliff Norton**

CL : **The X-Girl Clothing Company**

SIZE : **177 × 127mm**

アパレルメーカー　製品案内
Apparel Maker　Product Brochure
Brasil　1994

CD, AD, D : **Sérgio Liuzzi**

P : **Nana Moraes**

DF : **Interface Designers**

CL : **Andrea Saletto**

SIZE : **295 × 205mm**

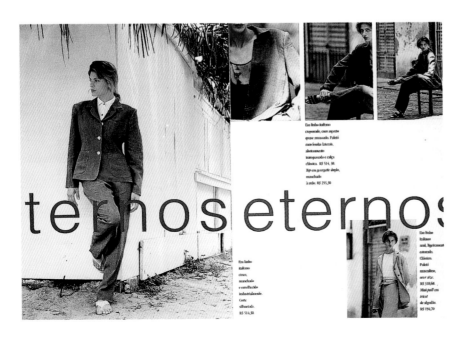

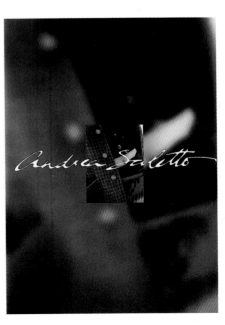

◀ WESTMINSTER

MINER'S PANT ▶

DRAY

◀ LAU

POACHER

アパレルメーカー　製品案内
Apparel Maker　Product Brochure
UK　1996

AD, D : **Alan Aboud**

P : **Saul Fletcher**

Brand Name : **R · Newbold**

SIZE : **270 × 279mm**

Corinne Sarrut

Corinne Sarrut

Corinne Sarrut

Corinne Sarrut

Corinne Sarrut

1

autumn whirl wind current style

essentials for the streamlined spi

2

3

1, 2. アパレルメーカー　製品案内　Apparel Maker　Product Brochures　Japan　1996
CD : Tamotsu Yagi　P : John Chan / Christiana Ceppas　DF : Tamotsu Yagi Design　CL : Tomorrowland Co., Ltd.　SIZE : 180 × 130mm

3. アパレルメーカー 製品案内 Apparel Maker Product Brochure Australia 1994
CD, D : **Fabio Ongarato** AD : **Fiona Scanlan** D : **Ronnen Goren** P : **Polly Borland** DF : **Fabio Ongarato Design** CL : **Scanlan & Theodore** SIZE : **148 × 105mm**

アパレルメーカー　プロモーション
Apparel Maker　Promotional Brochure
Italy　1995

CD, AD, D : **Giona Maiarelli**

P : **Alessandro Esteri**

CW : **Verdiana Maggiorelli**

DF : **Maiarelli & Rathkopf**

CL : **Lanificio del Casentino**

SIZE : **300 × 250mm**

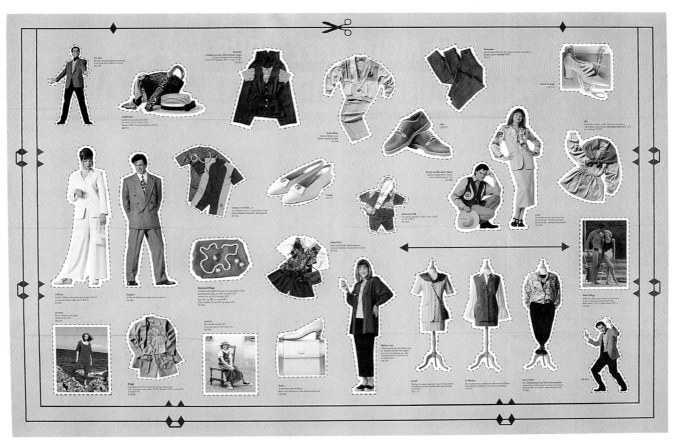

ショッピングセンター　商品案内　Shopping Center　Advertising Poster　Canada　1994
CD : Ghyslaine Fallu　AD : Jacqueline Zegray　D : André Renaud　P : Jean-François Brunelle　DF : Tam-Tam Inc.　CL : Place Vertu　SIZE : 223×153mm

ジーンズメーカー　ショップ案内
Jeans Maker　Flagship Store Guide
UK　1994

CD, I, CW : **Jeff Kindleysides**

D : **Carl Murch**

P : **Jon Arnold**

DF : **Checkland Kindleysides**

CL : **Levi Strauss（UK）Limited**

SIZE : **211 × 296mm**

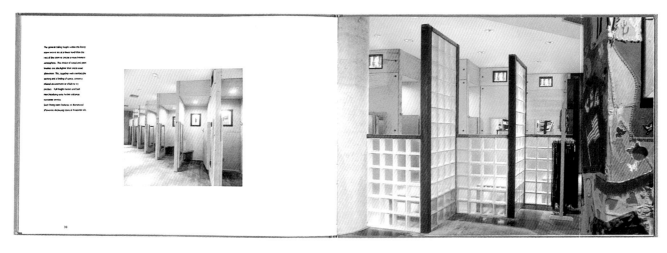

ma
che volete

queste cose
appartengono anche a loro

certamente non
appartengono a me

di mio ho solo

una camicia il **sax** e una pioggia di note

Jolie Francine,
petit femme

non ti ho
voluta
svegliare

perché non è ancora natale
e non lo sarà fino alle ore ventiquattro
non lo sarà finché sarò di nuovo con te

e se non ci sarai quando torno
non lo sarà affatto

(non me la sentivo di toglierti la mia camicia,
e poi la tua blusa mi dona)

アパレルメーカー　製品案内
Apparel Maker Product Brochure
Italy 1992

CD, AD, D : **Giona Maiarelli**

D : **Ann Rathkopf**

P : **Alessandro Esteri**

DF : **Maiarelli & Rathkopf**

for Euro Advertising

CL : **Alea**

SIZE : **325 × 325mm**

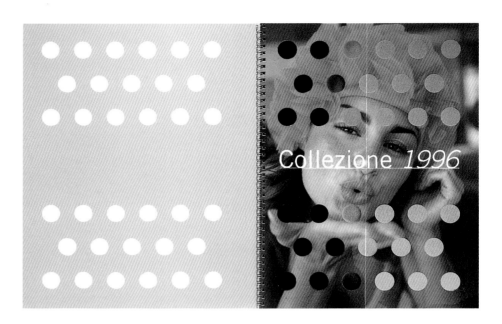

アパレルメーカー　製品案内
Apparel Maker　Product Catalogue
Italy　1995

CD, AD, D : **Giona Maiarelli**

CD : **Tiziano Campolmi**

P : **Peggy Sirota**

CW : **Rolando Dotti**

DF : **Maiarelli & Rathkopf for FCL**

CL : **Arcte**

SIZE : **360 × 275mm**

アパレルメーカー　製品案内
Apparel Maker　Product Brochure
Japan　1996

AD : **Soujiro Saito**

P : **Katsumi Omori**

CL : **Tsumori Chisato**

SIZE : **180×180mm**

SHOES
RULE
OK

アパレルメーカー　製品案内
Apparel Maker　Product Brochure
Italy　1996

CD : Elio Fiorucci

AD, P : Edland Man

D : Lorenzo dē Grassi

CL : Fiorucci S. R. L.

SIZE : 280 × 210mm

アパレルメーカー　製品案内
Apparel Maker　Product Brochure
Japan　1995

AD : **HAL**

D : **Shinji Abé**

P : **Ryu Tamagawa**

Hair & Make-up : **Kooki Taishima**

CL : **Betty's Blue**

SIZE : **297 × 210mm**

アパレルメーカー　製品案内
Apparel Maker　Promotional Brochure
Hong Kong　1993

CD, AD, D : Ching Lai Shan

P : Kam Ming NG

DF : Eye Studio Ltd.

CL : Pine Link Knitting Factory Ltd.

SIZE : 353 × 285mm

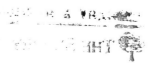

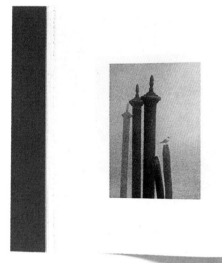

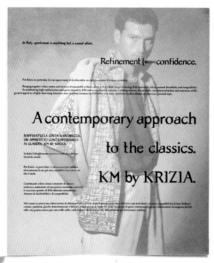

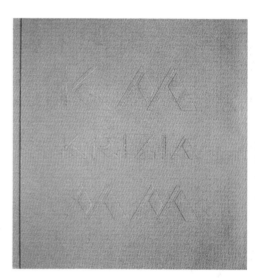

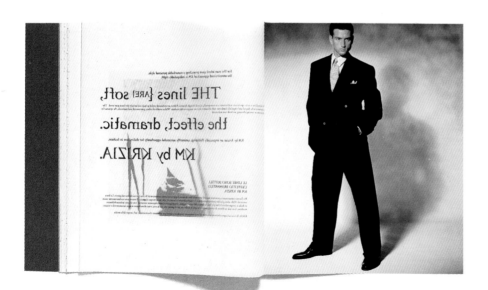

アパレルメーカー　製品案内
Apparel Maker　Product Brochure
USA　1995

CD, AD, D : **Carlos Segura**

DF : **Segura Inc.**

CL : **Krizia**

SIZE : **384 × 343mm**

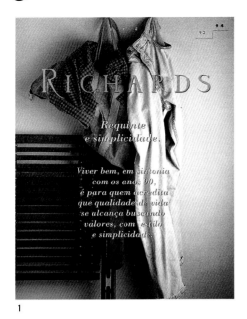

1

アパレルメーカー　製品案内
Apparel Maker　Product Brochures
Brasil　1994

CD, AD, D : **Sérgio Liuzzi**

CD, AD : **Ricardo Ferreira**

P : **Levindo Carneiro（1）/
Bettmann Archive（2）/ Nana Moraes（2）**

DF : **Interface Designers**

CL : **Richards**

SIZE : **275 × 210mm**

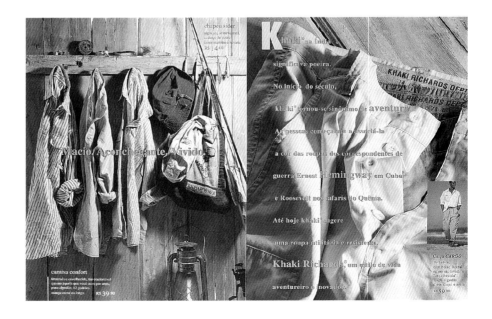

2

1

アパレルメーカー　製品案内
Apparel Maker　Product Brochures
Brasil　1994（1）1993（2）

CD, AD, D : **Sérgio Liuzzi / André de Castro**（2）

CD, AD : **Ricardo Ferreira**

P : **Nana Moraes**（1）/ **Levindo Carneiro**（2）

DF : **Interface Designers**

CL : **Richards**

SIZE : **275 × 210mm**

2

1996 SPRING COLLECTION

1996 SUMMER COLLECTION

1996 AUTUMN COLLECTION

アパレルメーカー　製品案内　Apparel Maker　Product Brochures　Japan　1996
CD：Mitsuhiko Irie　AD：Hideki Shimosako　P：Toshio Hagiri　CL：Powder Co., Ltd.　SIZE：250×210mm

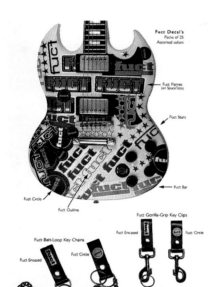

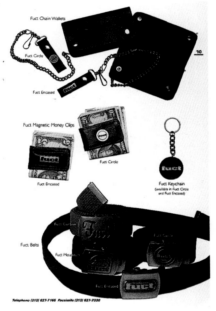

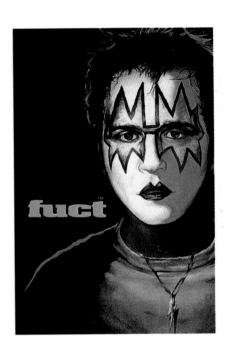

アパレルメーカー　製品案内
Apparel Maker　Product Catalogue
USA　1996

CD, AD, D : **Mark J. Leroy**

AD : **Erik Brunetti**

P : **Carey Hendricks Photography /
Edward Louderback**

I : **Richard Louderback**

DF : **Mark Designs**

CL : **Fuct™ Clothing Company, Inc.**

SIZE : **216 × 140mm**

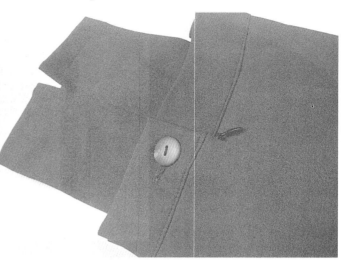

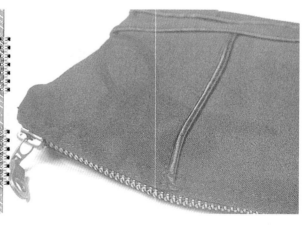

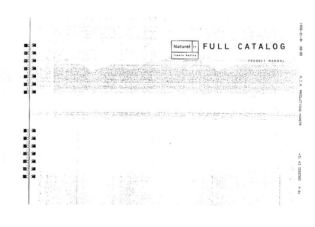

アパレルメーカー 製品案内
Apparel Maker Promotional Catalogue
The Netherlands 1995

CD, D : **Boy Bastiaens**

D : **Albert Kiefer**

P : **Marc Delahay**

CL : **M. J. M. Productions**

SIZE : **210 × 297mm**

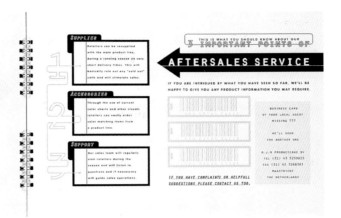

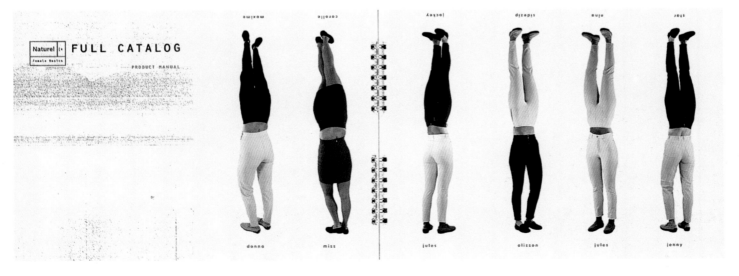

アパレルメーカー　製品案内
Apparel Maker　Product Brochure
UK　1996

AD : **Alan Aboud**

D : **Maxine Law**

P : **Karena Perronet Miller**

Brand Name : **Paul Smith**

SIZE : **362 × 256mm**

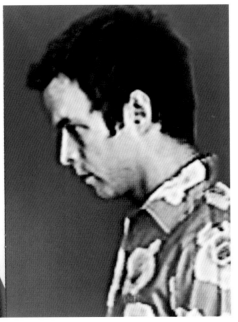

アパレルメーカー　製品案内
Apparel Maker　Product Brochure
UK　1996

AD, D：**Alan Aboud**

P：**Julian Broad**

Brand Name：**Paul Smith**

SIZE：**362 × 256mm**

go>SILK

アパレルメーカー　製品案内
Apparel Maker　Product Catalogue
USA　1993

AD : Laura Valenzuela

P : Jeffrey Barone

Typography : Robert Bentley

CL : Go>Silk

SIZE : 222 × 222mm

帽子メーカー　製品案内
Hat Maker　Product Brochure
USA　1993-1994

CD, AD : **Joe Vaughn**

D : **Jennifer Lundahl**

P : **Steve Nickerson**

CW : **Ron Lee**

DF : **Pipe Creative**

CL : **Boswell Millinery**

SIZE : **159 × 159mm**

s946

s947

s944

s945

s941

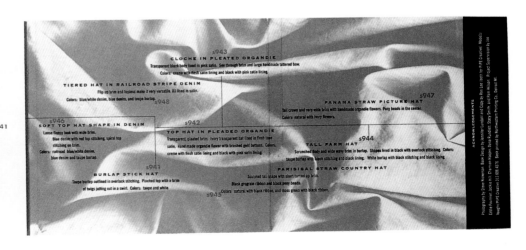

Our first range has been developed by listening to your requests and marrying ancient mythology with modern technology. Inspired by ancient philosophies of Gaylen and Hippocrates, the original alchemists of wax, essence and oils, we have reinterpreted ancient science resulting in haircare products that treat the heart, body and soul.

Kusco - Murphy Product available: Normal Hair Wash.

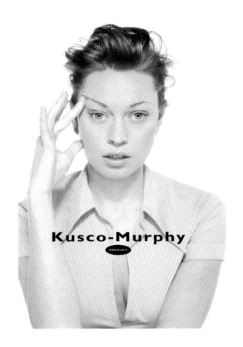

Enjoy the sensation of invigorating sea minerals, exotic essences and fragrant blossom every time you wash your hair. Kusco-Murphy are pleased to offer you indulgent personal care that embraces the purity of simplicity.

エステティックサロン　製品案内
Aesthetic Salon　Product Brochure
Australia　1995

CD, AD, D : **Fabio Ongarato**

D : **Tim Richardson**

P : **Greg Delves / Peter Rosetzky**

DF : **Fabio Ongarato Design**

CL : **Kusco-Murphy Pty Ltd.**

SIZE : **210 × 146mm**

Kusco-Murphy Products

Dry Wash:
A delicious combination of Camomile, Ylang Ylang and Jasmine that penetrates and nourishes hair cuticles giving lustre and strength to damaged hair.

Dry Rinse:
A moisturising conditioner that helps hydrate the hair shaft though an enriching blend of Camomile, Rose Hip and Ylang Ylang.

Dry Leave In:
A reconditioning treatment to nourish processed, dry and frizzy hair. Essence of Burdock, Orange Blossom and Camomile will collectively penetrate hair structure to restore health and shine. Simply spray onto wet or dry hair, set and go.

Normal Wash:
A re-balancing everyday shampoo that adds gloss and manageability. Contains Lime Blossom, Clary Sage and Lavender.

Normal Rinse:
A botanical bouquet of Lavender, Rosemary and Lime Blossom that sweetly scents and conditions the hair.

Oily Wash:
Cleanse hair with the invigorating fragrances of Sea Minerals, essences of Lemon and Sage. Adds volume and regulates oil.

Oily Leave In:
A refreshing treatment made out of plant and fruit extracts that freshen hair cuticles, with the medicinal benefits of Stinging Nettle, Burdock, Sage and Lemon Extract. Reduces scalp irritation while restoring life to limp hair. Simply spray onto wet or dry hair, set and go.

Lavender Hair Styling Cream:
A fragrant hair cream spiked with fresh Lavender Essence. It calms and moistens hair weightlessly. Set curly or sleek straight styles also an effective aid to control frizz and fly-away hair.

Cinnamon Hair Wax:
Perfumed with the aroma of cinnamon, a 100% natural beeswax that will firmly set and hold hair.

Setting Lotion:
All blossom pink setting lotion which is a healthy alternative to hairspray. A long lasting styling aid to hold curls in hot roller and wave sets, protects hair from the drying effects of blow waving.

Kusco - Murphy Product available: Setting Lotion.

化粧品メーカー　製品案内
**Cosmetics Manufacturer
Product Brochure**
UK　1996

AD : **Debbie Pike**

P : **Kerry Wilson / Francois Matyss**

CL : **Prestige Cosmetics**

SIZE : **148 × 210mm**

Where has your make-up taken you lately? If you are stuck in a beauty rut, it's time for a change. The secret to great looking make-up is prestige. Models, make-up artists and those in-the-know all swear by prestige. It's a capsule collection of fashionable lip and eye colours at no-nonsense prices.

It's no ordinary range there are over fifty lip colours and thirty eye colours to choose from which are designed to work in harmony. Prestige prides itself in innovative products, which give interesting finishes and offer more mileage than other ranges (the lippies work as great cheek bases and the eye preparations double as lip and brow definers). Prestige makes things happen, keeping you at the forefront of fashion and allows you to update your cosmetic bag as often as you like. For the low down on what's hot (and what's not) get ahead with prestige ...

THE TIMELESS CLASSIC

Directional looks which have literally become timeless beauty classics have been given the cosmetic equivalent to a face lift. At the catwalk collections the subtlest natural faces were updated with soft shades of pink, yellow and orange to achieve new radiance. Lips still remain sheer and pale. When selecting natural lipsticks look for colours which complement your skin tone; Cream, yellow or orange based shades for yellow skin tones and pinkey naturals for red or blue under-tones. Hot new shades for neo-natural eyes include prestige tender pink, mystic mauve and cashmere brown and soft options for the lips are prestige mocha, dune or toffee.

For a more dramatic finish team dark khol rimmed eyes with sheer berry toned lips.

Investment buys for the look include prestige wine lipstick liner, dubbonet long lasting lipstick, coffee eyeshadow and expresso eyeliner.

PERFECT THE LOOK···

Give make-up a professional finish and learn the tricks of the trade to transform day looks into instant evening glamour. Make the eyes the focal point of beauty. Sweep prestige classic pencil in granite along the socket and blend with the fingertips. Then dust prestige eyeshadow in chill onto the lid and brow bone. Add a slick of prestige automatic eyeliner (to make the task easier lift the eyelid at the brow with one finger and then apply in one stroke). Make-up artists always leave a subtle

top tricks

gap between the edge of the lashes and the line to make eyes appear bigger. Two coats of prestige long lash mascara are a must-have. Wipe the wand with a tissue before applying to prevent overloading the lashes. Team the eyes with subtley defined lips. First apply lipstick and then shade the outer corners of the lips with prestige automatic pencil (in a tone darker than your chosen lippie).

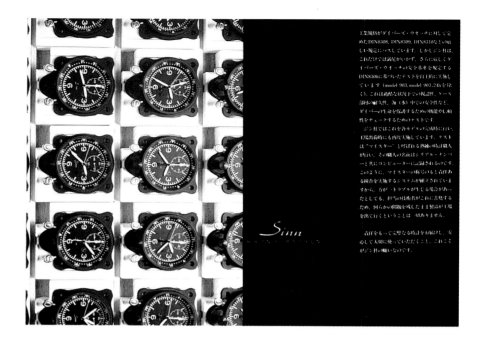

工業規格がダイバーズ・ウオッチに対して定めたDIN8308、DIN8309、DIN8310などの厳しい規定にパスしています。しかしジン社は、これだけでは満足がいかず、さらに厳しくダイバーズ・ウオッチの安全基準を規定するDIN8306に基づいたテストを自主的に実施しています（model 903、model 903.24hを除く）。これは過酷な状況下での視認性、ケース部品の耐久性、海（水）中での安全性など、ダイバーの生命を保護するための機能性や信頼性をチェックするためのテストです。

ジン社ではこれを各モデルの完成時に、1個消費毎にも再度実施しています。テストは"マイスター"と呼ばれる熟練の時計職人が担い、その職人の名前はシリアル・ナンバーと共にコンピューターに記録されるのです。このように、マイスターの検印いりとも言がある検査を実施するシステムが確立されていますから、万一トラブルが生じる場合があったとしても、担当の技術者がこれに善処するため、何らか問題を残したまま製品が工場を出て行くということは一切ありません。

高圧をもって完璧な時計をお届けし、安心して大切に使っていただくこと。これこそがジン社の願いなのです。

Sinn
WATCH CHRONOGRAPH

Sinn
CHRONOGRAPHEN

model 156.Bは1960年代に旧西ドイツ空軍に制式採用したmodel 155の後継モデルです。いささか奇妙な形状はパイロット用クロノグラフとして典型的ですが、これは実用上の理屈に基づづけられるものです。例えば、大型のベゼルは、夜光ベゼルは視認性の向上に役立つだけでなく、厚手のパイロット・グローブをつけた状態でも最易かつ確実に操作を行うための配慮でもあります。わがまに演画した強化加工のアクリル・ガラスは、メンテナンスを考慮して選択しました。極めて狭い戦闘機のコクピットでは、例えどんなに硬質の素材を用いても、腕時計の風防ガラスは必ずといっていいほど傷だらけになってしまいます。しかしアクリル・ガラスならば、ポリッシュ（磨くこと）によってこれを比較的簡単に復元することが可能です。ポリッシュのメンテナンスは室内側でも行えるため、使い慣れた時計を常に身近に置いておくことができるのです。ねじ込み式のリュウズも、単に防水性を向上させるためだけのものではありません。ケースやリュウズにかかった衝撃が、直接ムーブメントに影響するのを防ぐ役割も果たしています。

裏蓋には、ドイツ軍のミルスペックに基づいてmodel 155で開発した特殊ねじ止め構造を採用。これらすべての特徴を表現するものとして"MILITARY"の文字を立字にプリントしています。model 156.Bは、革のパイロットをはじめ多くの民間航空機のパイロットに愛用される伝統的なモデルです。

model 156.B

156.B
自動巻きクロノグラフ（Lemania5100/17石）
ステンレススチール・ケース（マット仕上げ）
直径43ミリ、防水・耐圧：10Bar
回転式ナビゲーション・ベゼル、2時間表示
60分積算計、12時間積算計、スモールセコンド
日付・曜日表示、強化アクリル・ガラス製風防
ねじ込み式リュウズ
ドイツ軍仕様特殊ステンレス・バック
アンチショック、アンチマグネティック
標準レザー・ストラップ（幅20ミリ）付き
価格15万5000円

model 903.24hは12時間表示式のmodel 903プロフェッショナル・ユースにするために、精製するレマニア社の手巻きクロノグラフ・ムーブメント"Cal. No. 1873"に改良を加え、24時間表示式にしたモデルです。通常の航海時計の時針は午前と午後で1日に文字盤を2周しますが、24時間表示式の場合は1日に1周で、例えば飛行中のパイロットが突天候に見舞われたとしましょう。地雷のたちこめる上空では飛行軸時刻が"長時間"に並べづらいほど、自身の判断や判断によって変化もっとなっています。なんらかのトラブルが発生し管制塔との交信が不可能となった場合では、なおさら弧軍になる現実に帰りがちなのです。文字盤を見ただけで瞬時に昼夜の判別がでる24時間表示式式時刻針を使用することは、これを回避するために有効な手段です。文字盤のインディックスは、12時間表示式での時針の位置に12の数字を配しています。これによって文字盤上部は昼間、下部は夜間と、ひと目で判断ができるのです。また、時差さえ把握していれば、回転ベゼルの操作によって目的地の現在時刻を知ることもできるという特徴も備えています。

model 903.24hでは、パイロット・クロノグラフに継承される基本的なデザインと機能はそのままに、時刻表示の方法だけを2時間式に変更。スペックとレザー・ストラップのカラーリングは、12時間表示式のモデルに準じています。

model 903.ST.GL.24h

model 903.PL.GL.24h

903.ST.GL.24h
24時間表示手巻きクロノグラフ（Lemania1877/18石）
ステンレススチール・ケース（ポリッシュ仕上げ）
直径40ミリ、日常生活防水
ナビゲーション用スライド・ルール（回転計算尺）
30分積算計、12時間積算計、スモールセコンド
ミネラル・ガラス製風防
ねじ込み式シースルー・バック（ミネラル・ガラス）
アンチショック、アンチマグネティック
標準レザー・ストラップ（幅22ミリ）付き
価格26万円

903.PL.GL.24h
24時間表示手巻きクロノグラフ（Lemania1877/18石）
ステンレススチール・ケース（ゴールドプレイテッド）
直径40ミリ、日常生活防水
ナビゲーション用スライド・ルール（回転計算尺）
30分積算計、12時間積算計、スモールセコンド
ミネラル・ガラス製風防
ねじ込み式シースルー・バック（ミネラル・ガラス）
アンチショック、アンチマグネティック
標準レザー・ストラップ（幅22ミリ）付き
価格28万円

時計輸入販売会社　商品案内
Watch Distributor　Product Brochure

Japan　1995

CL：**PX Incorporated**

SIZE：**210 × 148mm**

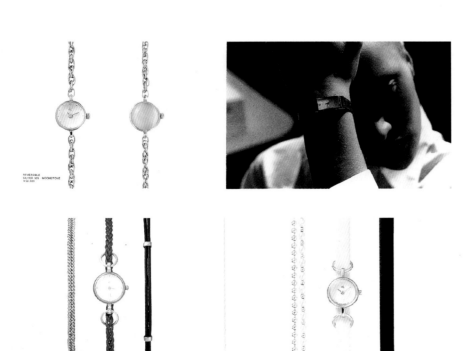

アクセサリー / アパレルメーカー　製品案内
Accessories / Apparel Maker
Product Brochures
Japan　1996

CD, DF : **Yumiko Hisanaga**

P : **Junai Nakagawa**

DF : **Vie. Inc.**

CL : **4℃**

SIZE : **187 × 98mm**

1

2

1. メガネフレームメーカー 製品案内 Eyewear Frame Manufacturer Product Catalogue Australia 1994
AD: Annette Harcus D: Stephanie Martin P: Petrina Tinslay CW: Philip Bradshaw DF: Harcus Design CL: Jonathan Sceats Eyewear SIZE: 101×210mm

2. アクセサリー／アパレルメーカー 製品案内 Accessories / Apparel Maker Product Catalogue USA 1995
AD. D: Jack Anderson D: David Bates P: Darrell Peterson I: Todd Connor CW: Julie Huffaker DF: Hornall Anderson Design Works, Inc. CL: Sun Dog, Inc. SIZE: 216×140mm

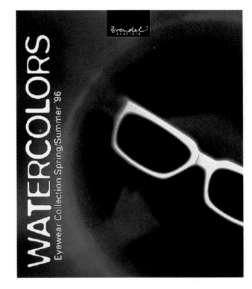

メガネメーカー　製品案内
Eyeglass Manufacturer
Product Brochure
Germany　1995

CD. CW : **Olíver Rach**

AD : **Ruediger Henning**

D : **Ann-Kristin Brendel**

P : **Christian Barth**

DF : **Halli Galli Design**

CL : **Brendel Lunettes**

SIZE : **285 × 231mm**

53717 CLA

CLASSIC

CLASSIC

26651 LEO

camaleón

15759 LEO

an **Urban**
shoe from
Camper

C Runner Mix

靴メーカー　製品案内
Shoe Manufacturer　Product Brocure
Spain　1996

CD : **Neville Brody**

CL : **Camper**

SIZE : **124 × 139mm**

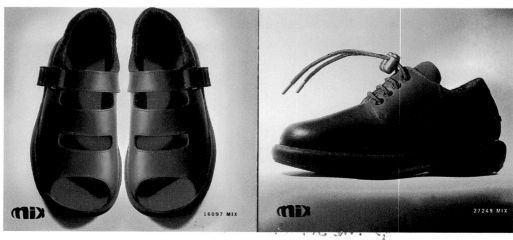

16097 MIX

27249 MIX

時計メーカー　製品案内
**Watch Manufacturer
Product Brochure**
Switzerland　1995

CL : Swatch S. A.

SIZE : **273×132mm**

1

2

3

アクセサリーメーカー　製品案内
Accessories Manufacturer
Product Brochures
Italy　1995-1996

CD : Monica Sarti

AD, CW : Columbus B. B.

AD : Bond Bonarelli

D : Monica Alisina

P : Claudio Minenti

DF, CL : Faliero Sarti Accessorio

SIZE : 330×224mm（1）/ 235×169mm（2）/
250×203mm（3）

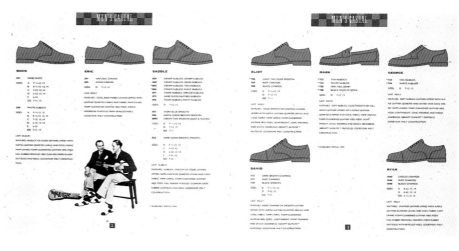

靴メーカー　製品案内
Shoe Manufacturer　Wholesale Catalogue
USA　1993

CD, AD, D, CW : **Leslie Evans**

AD, D : **Mary Brown**

D : **Cheryl Bryant**

P : **Carl Hyatt / George Benington**

I : **Ray Ciemny**

DF : **Leslie Evans Design Assoc.**

CL : **Geo. E. Keith, Co.**

SIZE : **228 × 230mm**

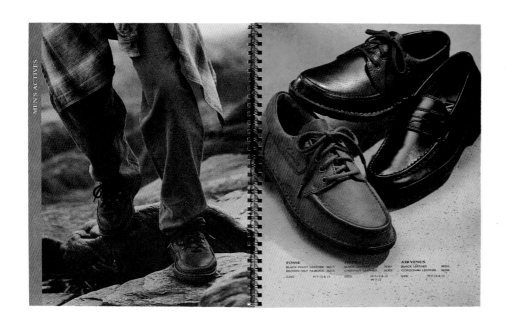

靴メーカー　製品案内
Shoe Manufacturer　Wholesale Catalogue
USA　1993

CD, AD, D : Leslie Evans

D : Cheryl Bryant

P : Angela Coppola / George Benington

CW : M. L. Hedison

Stylist : Barbara Kurgan

Printer : Penmor Lithographer

DF : Leslie Evans Design Assoc.

CL : Clarks of England

SIZE : 280×126mm

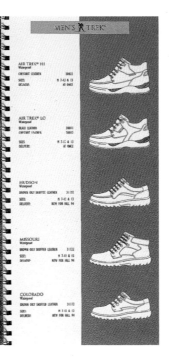

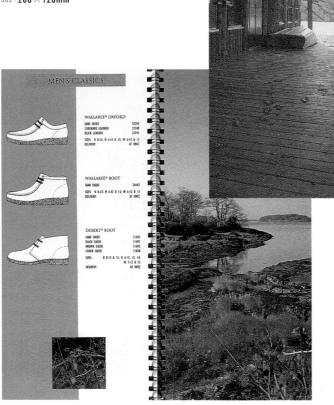

靴メーカー　製品案内
Shoe Manufacturer　Wholesale Catalogue
USA　1993

CD, AD, D, P : Leslie Evans

D : Cheryl Bryant

CW : Chris Kast

Printer : Penmor Lithographers

DF : Leslie Evans Design Assoc.

CL : Clarks of England

SIZE : 280×215mm

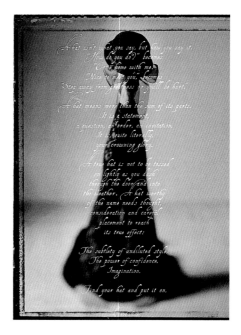

帽子メーカー　製品案内
Hat Maker　Product Brochure
USA　1996

CD, AD, D : **Carlos Segura**

P : **Jeff Sciortino**

CW : **Jim Marcus / Anna McCalister**

DF : **Segura Inc.**

CL : **Maramara**

SIZE : **201×140mm**

靴メーカー　ショップマニュアル
Shoe Manufacturer　Store Manual
UK　1995

D：Matthew Fawell
P：Jon Arnold
DF：Checkland Kindleysides
CL：Airwair
SIZE：208 × 304mm

One small step

One giant leap

調理收斂系列

潔膚調理液 LOTION CAPUCINE

含金盞花、富有效的完成完整之清潔效益、感覺清新舒適、去除殘留潔膚乳及皮膚表面之較大油性分子、紓緩活性型胞間質顆粒被皮膚吸收、塗抹調理乳收歛、含抗基礎能紓解皮膚刺激、促進血液循環使皮膚呈現色澤健康並快速吸收保養品平衡皮膚鬆弛現象、適用於肌纖類型肌膚、於開關使用潔膚乳後置於棉片上、輕擦臉部及頸部、以達到完美潔膚效果。

主成份：金盞花萃取、張力活性因子、胺基酸、矢車菊
編號：032201　容量：250ml　圖 1　□○⑤NC⦿●

柔軟調理液 LES INTEMPORELLES

不含酒精、富有效的完成完整之清潔效益、使皮膚感受清爽舒適、對乾燥敏感過敏肌膚產生之緊繃及病理象能立即紓緩、熱泉、並去除潔膚乳之後留不潔物及皮膚面層大油性分子、促進保品活性胞顆粒分子源料吸收、含尿素素促使肌膚柔軟、再生、催化血液循環色澤健康、平衡反應型胞維、適用於乾燥、敏感性肌膚、於開關使用潔膚乳後置於棉片上、輕擦臉部、頸部、以達完美潔膚效果。

主成份：鱷梨、尿素素、羽毛草、金盞菊、早金蓮
編號：042201　容量：250ml　圖 2　□○⑤NC⦿＋

防護收斂液 LOTION TONIQUE JONQUILLE

不含酒精、富有調養皮膚活動力、立即達膚效果、紓緩皮膚天然保濕層、兼具抗菌作用、增加抵禦外界侵襲能力、有效給予肌層水份之滋養、刺激皮膚彈性、使毛孔收斂、紓助化妝持久輕除皮膚鬆弛反應、適用各類霜晚層於早上潔膚皮膚後置於棉片上輕拍臉部及頸部、再配合日霜。

主成份：黃木蘭萃取、薄荷葉、茉衣草、定龍
編號：034201　容量：250ml　圖 3　□○⑤NC⦿＋

柔紋收斂液 LOTION TONIQUE

不含酒精、溫和的滋養皮膚活動力、立即達膚效果、使毛孔收斂、增加彈性、使化妝持久、兼具安定舒爽、補充皮膚水分、感覺細嫩、舒爽、視覺細緻抗油性同與皮膚的外界抗壓力、防止雙油乾破裂、輕除皮膚常反應皮膚過敏性鬆弛、紅印明紓於早上清潔皮膚後置於棉片上輕拍臉部、頸部消和配合日霜。

上成份：廈香萃取、甜沒藥、紅寬葡素、坡尿酸
編號：043201　容量：250ml　圖 4　□○⑤NC⦿

油性面皰系列

酵素淨膚組 FORMULE EFFERVESCENTE

針對油性問題膚質所產生之粉刺、毛孔阻塞物、進行溫和面有效的溶解性治療、利用蛋白酵素之分解作用、廉膚膿狀彈深除毛孔中不潔物排出之粉刺、量晶靈皮因適克擠壓造成之出血、凹凸問題更深、只克象作用、使毛孔潔淨後立即緊貼著重建皮膚正常pH值幫助去除老死細胞功能、使肌膚潔淨、柔軟、易於吸收治療性保養品、神奇功收紓緩使用6次即暖膚活力功效、於表皮接膚產或膚部、特觸末面泥小面中（全臉 包、局部半包、背部二包）以 包基合 小格型的液態適合調勻、再連生泡床、用卻干脂泡沫網至思處或全檢、用、5層膜以水沖淨、適用油性肌膚或一般肌膚阻刺現象之局部、視毛孔狀況隔週使用1~2次。

主成份：粉末－滾粉末、蛋白酵素、金鍍腸、趨電油　潔腸－檸檬酸、發酵因子
編號：137600　容量：1.5g糊x e包·50ml液體膜　圖 4　□○⑤NC⦿＋

活性酵素面膜 MASQUE EXPRESS

黑濃型快速膜、具活化摩末能廉凝分解毛孔中不潔物使毛孔潔淨、激勵皮膚收歛作用、使毛孔收緩細質、含天然保濕因子立即賦充皮膚水份、使感受柔軟清新更具光澤、海海連抹輕素擦摩輕鬆層、強晶帶晶3分鐘脫以水沖淨、內配合清真調理素、適用混合性、油性膚質、每星期可他使、3次。

主成份：金澤柏、葡萄油、木瓜酵素、保濕因子
編號：138200　容量：5cml　圖 5　□○⑤V⒞⦿＋

嫩白抗皺系列

嫩白抗皺日霜 STRATEGIE JEUNESSE

榮譽前緻活性配方、針對工作、情緒壓力敏大的成女前設計、實有效在皮膚表面刺眼嫩復緊固保護紋、抵抗氣惡、空氣污染、冷熱溫差、並促進微循環管加速循環、使膚色黑潤、加速新陳代謝、促進再生作用、改善皮膚不美麗的黯黑使膚色紅潤白、微粒活性或份能加深層補充營份、使肌膚恢復活力、防止狀壓力的問題的之鬆弛、細紋現象、長期使用能使皮膚腫滋柔軟、嫩白、返印的消反、可直接作化收嫩膚霜、適用於成青年部5歲以上、黑斑、職業鍵老之各類敏感皮膚、早上塗抹於嫩淨膚後的臉部、頸部。

主成份：動物腸膜萃取素、水份子複合素、胺基酸、陽光折射元素　絲蛋白、玻尿酸、防止壓力氣合物、屬紫菊、山茶甘油
編號：122600　容量：30ml　圖 4　□○⑤NC⦿＋

嫩白抗皺晚霜 STRATEGIE JEUNESSE NUIT

這是一種具三階段抗老化功能的多重效果密集補霜、這養多元化不鬆馳、第一階段：去除細胞內壞死的作用、催化迴腸復殘部之組立作用、使肌膚更新代謝功能、輕層累積膚物、氣合作用正常、加速新陳膜生成、幫助防止肌膚出現老死現象、第二階段：活化肌膚老濃的功能：因食活化生物素之、飲譽與活性或份能深層補進、持續大活動力、增加皮膚抗力、減少過敏、第三階段：使肌膚自我修護能力的回復、強化膠原膜廉的網狀組織、抑帶理是維的緊固活化能力、去除細鬆老化現象、除三階的密集效果外益含粉紅色調節天然保濕因子、這到調層精給水效果、使肌膚活性柔滑、舒適長期使用能提供柔固保護滑層、柔滑、年輕、彈性、約緻狀態、適用於抗皺、職業婦女3以上的各類型霜、膚、鬆弛達抹於臉部、頸部、輕加按摩、頸部。

主成份：動物腸膜萃取素、胺基素、玻尿酸、絲蛋白、活化生物廉能結A.E.F.、荷荷芭油、天然現因子
編號：013100　容量：50ml　圖 5　□○⑤NC⦿＋

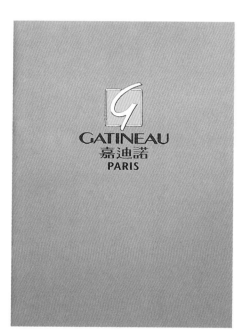

GATINEAU
嘉迪諾
PARIS

化粧品販売会社　商品案内
Cosmetics Agency　Product Brochure
Taiwan　1994

CD, AD : Raymond Lam

D : Stephen Lau / Vivian Yao

P : Dynasty Photography

DF : Artailor Design House（TPE）

CL : Cosactive & Jefferey Co., Ltd.

SIZE : 240 × 165mm

化粧品メーカー　製品案内
Cosmetics Company　Presentation Kit
Italy　1994

CD. D : **Giorgio Rocco**

CW : **Anna Andreuzzi**

DF : **Giorgio Rocco Communications
Design Consultants**

P. CL : **L'Oréal**

SIZE : **297 × 210mm**

ジュエリーデザイナー　製品案内
Jewelry Designer　Product Brochure
The Netherlands　1992

CD, D : Henrik Barends

P : Tono Stano

DF : Studio Henrik Barends

CL : Ruudt Peters

SIZE : 145×105mm

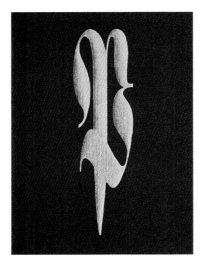

ジュエリーデザイナー　製品案内
Jewelry Designer　Product Brochure
Belgium / The Netherlands　1995

CD, D : Henrik Barends

P : Winnifred Limburg

DF : Studio Henrik Barends

CL : Annemie de Corte

SIZE : 160×100mm

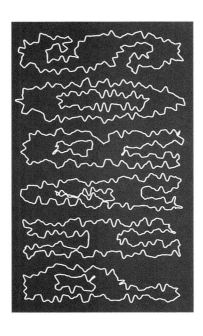

ジュエリーデザイナー　製品案内
Jewelry Designer　Product Brochure
The Netherlands　1995

CD, D : Henrik Barends

P : Winnifred Limburg

DF : Studio Henrik Barends

CL : Ruudt Peters

SIZE : 145×105mm

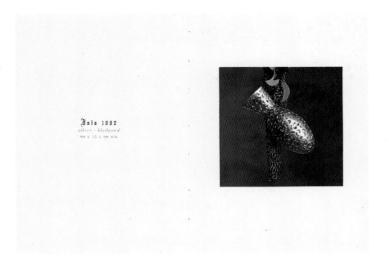

Isis 1992
zilver · bladgoud
90 X 13 X 90 MM

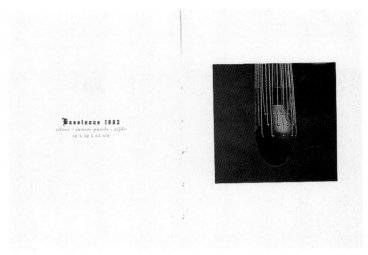

Bassinus 1992
zilver · zwarte parels · zijde
42 X 42 X 115 MM

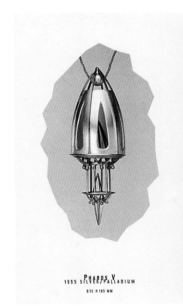

Pharos X
1995 SILVER/PALLADIUM
Ø35 H 105 MM

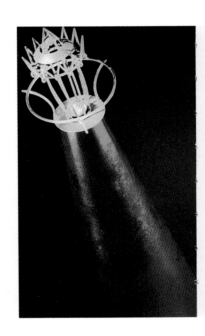

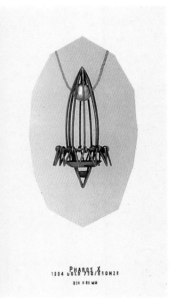

Pharos X
1994 GOLD 750/BRONZE
Ø34 H 90 MM

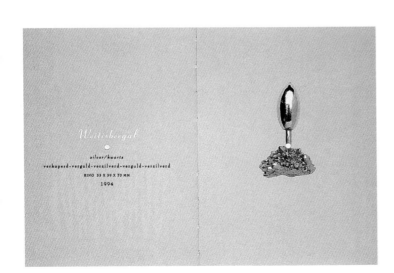

Weitisbergal
zilver/kwarts
verkoperd-verguld-verzilverd-verguld-verzilverd
RING 33 X 39 X 70 MM
1994

Wunstorf
zilver/marcasiet
bladgoud
RING 32 X 40 X 104 MM
1994

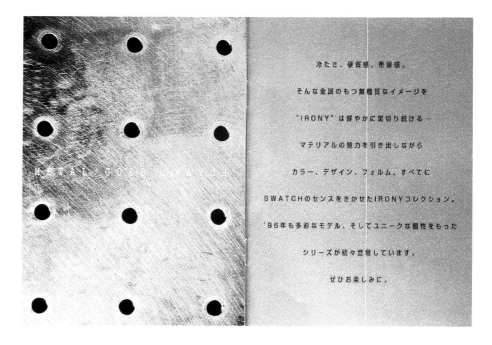

冷たさ、硬質感、衝撃感。

そんな金属のもつ無機質なイメージを

"IRONY" は鮮やかに裏切り続ける—

マテリアルの魅力を引き出しながら

カラー、デザイン、フォルム、すべてに

SWATCHのセンスをきかせたIRONYコレクション。

'96年も多彩なモデル、そしてユニークな個性をもった

シリーズが続々登場しています。

ぜひお楽しみに。

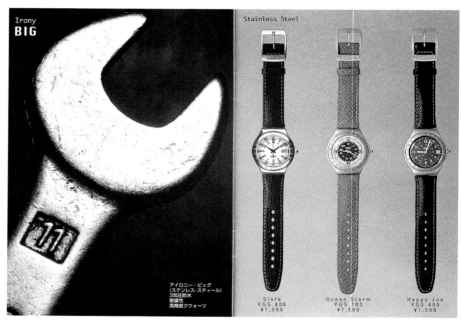

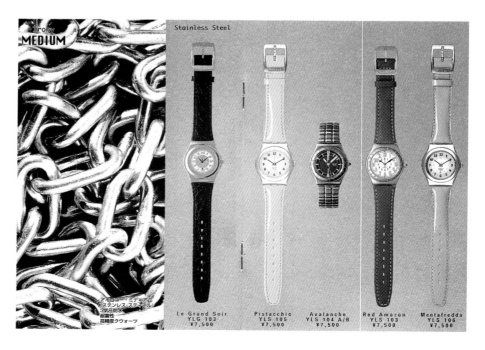

時計メーカー　製品案内
Watch Manufacturer　Product Brochure
Switzerland　1996

CL : Swatch S. A.

SIZE : 148 × 105mm

ゴルフクラブメーカー　製品案内　Golf Club Manufacturer　Product Brochure　USA　1994
CD, AD, D : **José Serrano** P : **Marshall Harrington** CW : **John Robertson / Joe Lazo** DF : **Mires Design, Inc.** CL : **Odyssey Golf** SIZE : **177 × 291mm**

スポーツウェアメーカー　製品案内
Sportswear Manufacturer
Product Brochure
USA　1990

CD, AD, D, CW：**Mike Salisbury**

D, I, CW：**Terry Lamb**

P：**Mike Funk**

I：**Patrick O'neal / Pam Hamilton /
Pat Linse / Elizabeth Salisbury**

DF：**Mike Salisbury Communications Inc.**

CL：**Gotcha**

SIZE：**303 × 266mm**

スポーツウェアメーカー　製品案内
Sportswear Manufacturer
Product Brochure
USA　1990

CD, AD, D：Mike Salisbury

P：Mike Funk

I：Pat Linse / Terry Lamb

DF：Mike Salisbury Communications Inc.

CL：Gotcha

SIZE：365×252mm

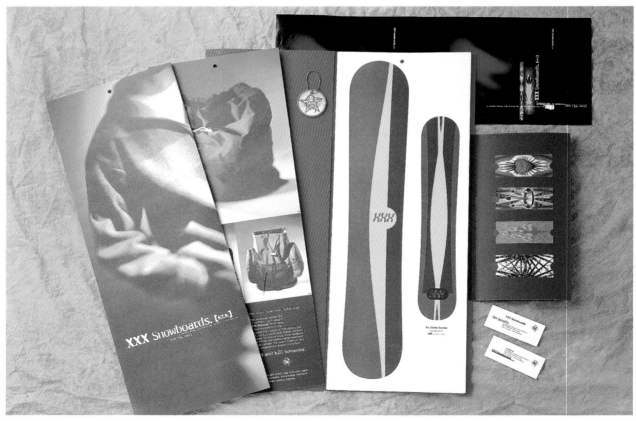

スノーボードメーカー　製品案内　Snowboard Manufacturer　New Product Announcements　USA　1995
CD, AD, D, I : Carlos Segura　P : Jeff Scintiono　I : Tony Klassen　DF : Segura Inc.　CL : XXX Snowboards　SIZE : 586 × 222mm

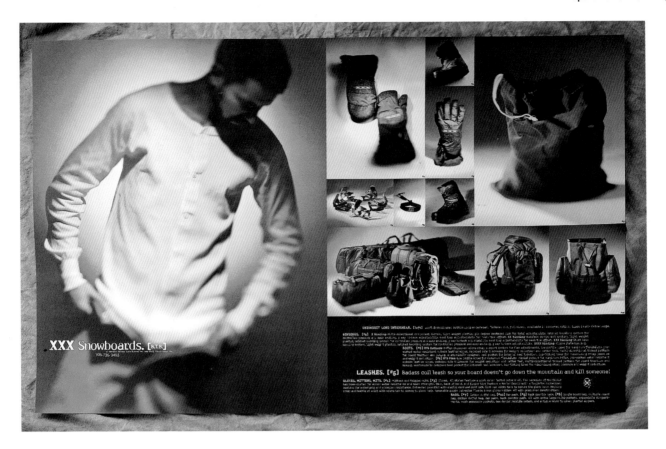

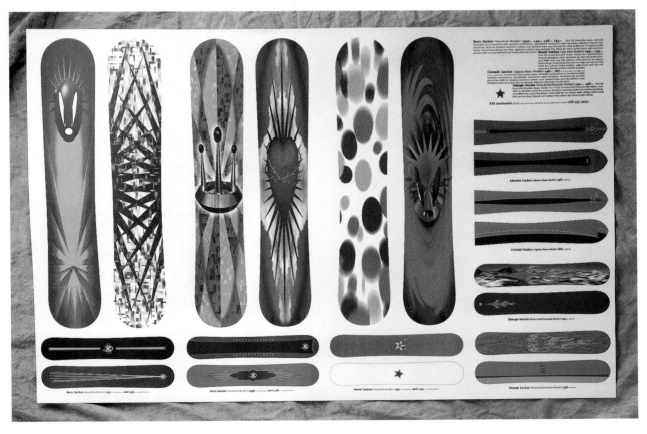

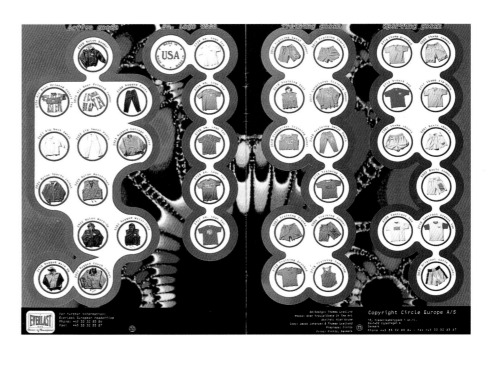

スポーツウェアメーカー　製品案内
Sportswear Manufacturer　Product Brochure
Denmark　1993

AD, D : **Thomas Lystlund**

P : **Sten Trolle**

CW : **Dalob Dohanzen**

CL : **Everlast**

SIZE : **420 × 297mm**

スイムスーツメーカー　製品案内
Swimwear Maker　Sales Brochures
Brasil　1995

CD, AD, D : **Sergio Steuer**

P : **Valério Trabanco**

DF : **D・Vision**

CL : **Cia. Marítima**

SIZE : **300 × 255mm**

自転車関連用品メーカー　製品案内
Bicycle Accessories Manufacturer
Product Catalogue
USA　1994

AD, D : Jack Anderson

D : David Bates / Mary Chin Hutchison

DF : Hornall Anderson Design Works, Inc.

CW, CL : Giro Sport Design, Inc.

SIZE : **136 × 216mm**

スポーツウェアメーカー　製品案内　Sportswear Maker　Product Brochure　USA　1994
AD, D：Jack Anderson　DF：Hornall Anderson Design Works, Inc.　CW, CL：Adidas　SIZE：279×215mm

ラケットボールメーカー　情報誌
**Racquetball Equipment / Apparel Maker
Information Magazines**
USA　1994（Page 78）　1992（Page 79）

CD, AD, D : **José Serrano**

P : **Carl Vanderschuit**

DF : **Mires Design, Inc.**

CL : **Ektelon**

SIZE : **280 × 216mm**

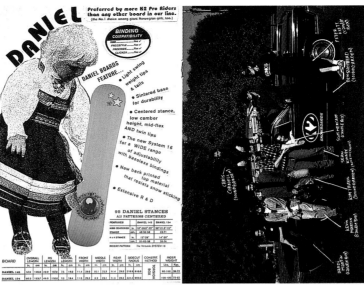

1. スノーボードメーカー　製品案内
**Snowboard Manufacturer
Promotional Brochure**
USA　1995

CD: Brent / Luke / Hayley

AD, D, I, CW: Michael Strassburger

D, I, CW: Robynne Raye / Vittorio Costarella /
George Estrada

P: Eric Berger / Jeff Curtes / Aarron Sedway /
Jimmy Clarke / Reuben Sanchez

DF: Modern Dog

CL: K2 Snowboards

SIZE: 208 × 137mm

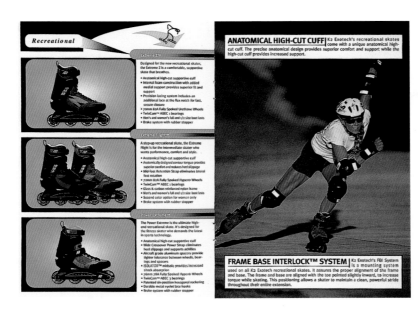

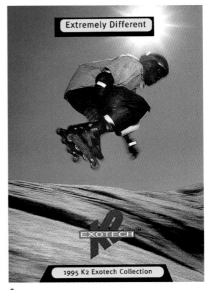

2

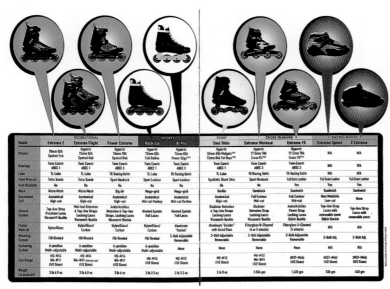

2. インラインスケートメーカー　製品案内
In-Line Skate Manufacturer　Product Brochure
USA　1994

CD, AD, D, I : **Michael Strassburger**

CD, AD : **Robynne Raye**

P : **Jeff Curtes / Scott Markowitz**

DF : **Modern Dog**

CL : **K2 Skates**

SIZE : **203 × 138mm**

3. インラインスケートメーカー　製品案内
In-Line Skate Manufacturer
Product Brochure
USA　1995

CD : **Shenna Fitzgerald**

AD, D, I : **George Estrada**

P : **Scott Markewitz / Jeff Curtes /
Greg Montijo**

DF : **Modern Dog**

CW, CL : **K2 Skates**

SIZE : **141 × 210mm**

Il R.R.D. è un nuovo dipartimento che da poco ha preso vita all'interno di NIKE Italy. Se dovessimo idealmente identificarlo all'interno della struttura aziendale lo dovremmo posizionare tra il settore Vendite e quello Marketing; è però a quest'ultimo che appartiene.

Cos'è il Retail Resources Department?

Se volessimo tradurre fedelmente il nome del dipartimento dovremmo chiamarlo "Dipartimento Risorse alle Vendite", denominazione che esprime perfettamente lo scopo del R.R.D.: **OFFRIRE AI CLIENTI NIKE E AL SETTORE VENDITE UN SUPPORTO** ed un servizio affinché il prodotto sia sempre appetibile.

Qual è il suo obiettivo?

Stimolare la domanda del consumatore e facilitare la vendita dei prodotti NIKE all'interno del punto vendita, attraverso l'allacciamento di relazioni a lungo termine e reciprocamente proficue con dettaglianti selezionati.

In pratica questo avviene grazie alla sinergia che intercorre tra le divisioni Ekin, Merchandising ed il supporto Retail Marketing/COOP Advertising (pubblicità con il rivenditore), le quali offrono rispettivamente un servizio di informazione tecnica, un servizio di visual merchandising ed un supporto espositivo e di salvaguardia del marchio all'interno del responsabile del R.R.D., il ha il preciso compito di ed attualmente segue, Manager, la progettazione singolo punto vendita. Il Retail Resources Manager, coordinare queste divisioni insieme al Merchandising e l'apertura dei NIKE Shop.

Cosa sono i NIKE Shop?

Town, sono il massimo (dal di immagine e di scelta) base per una solida Formato da strutture Area, il NIKE Shop permette rispettando al 100% i criteri enfatizzazione del

I NIKE Shop, dopo NIKE punto di vista espositivo, che NIKE possa offrire come partnership con il cliente, diverse rispetto alle NIKE di esporre le collezioni NIKE di esposizione e di prodotto.

By "R·R·D"
(Retail Resources Dept.)

3

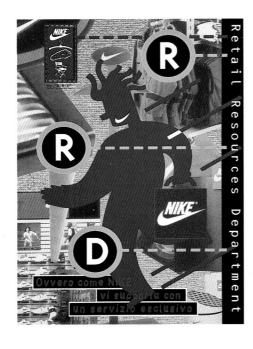

Retail Resources Department

Ovvero come Nike vi supporta con un servizio esclusivo

Nike Shop attuale

I NIKE Shop fin ora aperti in Italia (l'immagine sopra ne è un esempio). Nella foto accanto, i nuovi NIKE Shop, di cui troverete dettagli nelle pagine seguenti.

4

(in futuro)

I nuovi NIKE Shop disponibili da gennaio '96

5

スポーツ用品メーカー　ショップ案内
Sporting Goods Manufacturer
Retail Resources Brochure
Italy　1995

CD, AD : **Giampiero Gerbella**

I : **Barbara Casadei**

CL : **Nike Italy**

SIZE : **286 × 205mm**

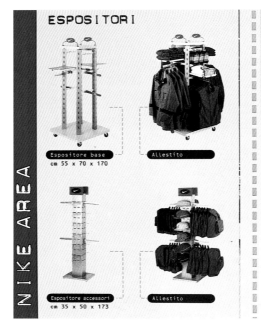

ESPOSITORI

NIKE AREA

Espositore base
cm 55 x 70 x 170

Allestito

Espositore accessori
cm 35 x 50 x 173

Allestito

Merchandising Department

Ekin Department

Retail Marketing

By "R·R·D"
(Retail Resources Dept.)

13

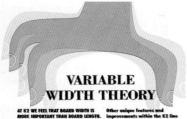

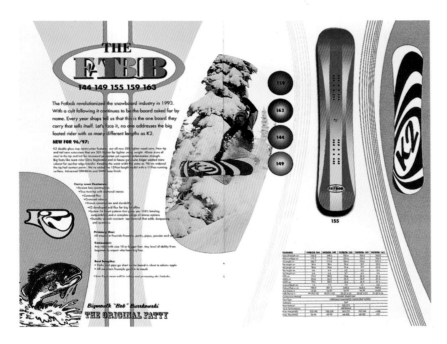

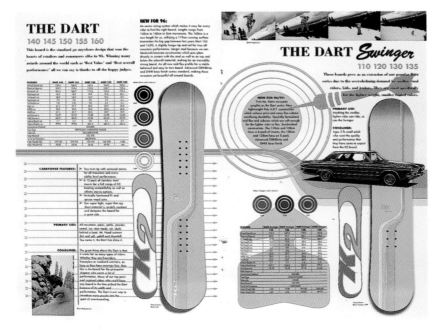

スノーボードメーカー　製品案内
Snowboard Manufacturer
Promotional Brochure
USA　1995

CD, CW : **Hayley Martin**

AD, D, I : **Michael Strassburger**

D, I : **Robynne Raye / Vittorio Costarella / George Estrada / Coby Schultz**

P : **Sean Sullivan / Jeff Curtes / Eric Berger**

CW : **Luke Edgar**

DF : **Modern Dog**

CL : **K2 Snowboards**

SIZE : **292 × 191mm**

BREAKING AWAY

ひとつのものを全部分解して、それをまた組立てる。私はそんな子供だった。14歳のころには、バイクショップで「Stingray」や「Peapickers」を組み合わせていた。そして20歳の頃には、最初のカチゴリ・ライダーになっていた。私の名は「Breaking Away」という映画。私そのもののストーリーだと感じたものだ。

PROCALIBER プロカリバー

KLUNKER クランカー

GEAR ギア

自転車販売会社　商品案内
Bicycle Distibutor　Product Brochure
USA / Japan　1996

CL : **Gary Fisher / FET Co., Ltd.**

SIZE : **275 × 212mm**

スポーツウェアメーカー　製品案内
Sportswear Manufacturer　Product Brochure
UK　1992

D : Richard Whitmore

P : Ronald Diltoer

I : Marian Sheppard

DF : Checkland Kindleysides

CL : Fred Perry Sportswear UK Ltd.

SIZE : 298×219mm

自転車用ヘルメットメーカー　製品案内　**Bicycle Helmet Manufacturer　Product Catalogue**　USA　1995
CD, AD : **José Serrano**　P : **Carl Vanderschuit**　CW : **John Kuraoka**　DF : **Mires Design, Inc.**　CL : **Proaction**　SIZE : **300×222mm**

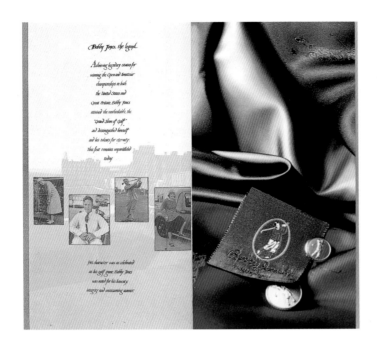

スポーツウェアー輸入販売会社　展示会カタログ
Sportswear Trading Company
Trade Exhibition Brochure
Hong Kong　1995

CD, AD, D : **Grand So**

AD, D : **Kwong Chi Man / Raymond Au**

P : **David Lo（Studio Rad）**

I : **James Fong**

DF : **Masterline Communications Ltd.**

CW, CL : **Ryoden Sports Ltd.**

SIZE : **355 × 224mm**

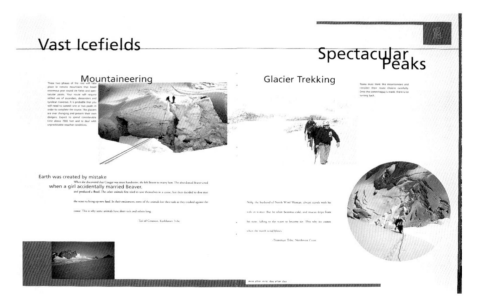

スポーツイベントスポンサー　イベント案内
Sporting Event Sponsor　Event Promotion
USA　1995

CD, AD, CW : Richard Seireeni

D : Jim Pezzullo

P : Kerry Phillips / Scott Flavelle /

　　Tourism B. C.

I : Tanja Richter

CW : Mark Burnett / James Pezzullo

DF : Studio Seireeni

CL : Eco-Challenge Lifestyles Inc.

SIZE : 290 × 230mm

水着メーカー　製品案内
Swimwear Maker Promotional Brochure
Sweden / USA 1993

CD, AD, D : **Richard Seireeni**

P : **John Colao**

DF : **Studio Seireeni**

CL : **Scandinavian Beachwear AB**

SIZE : **317 × 240mm**

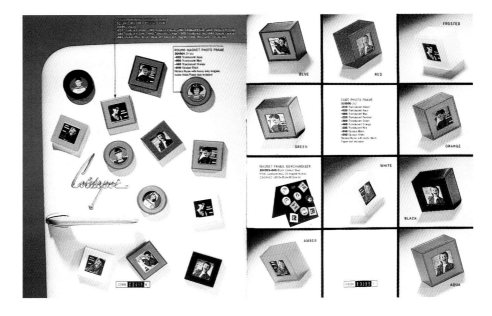

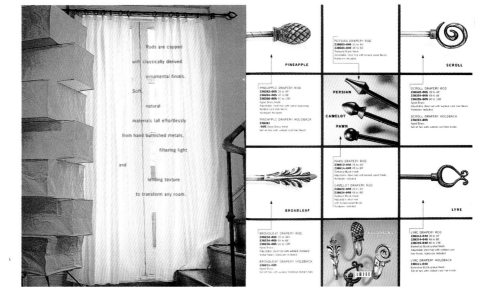

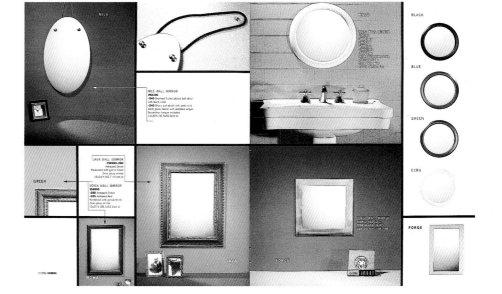

雑貨メーカー　製品案内
**Housewares Manufacturer
Supplementary Sales Catalogue**
USA / Canada　1996

CD, AD, D : **Claudia Neri**

P : **Chris Barnes / Graham Iddon**

DF : **Teikna**

CW, CL : **Umbra Ltd.**

SIZE : **280 × 210mm**

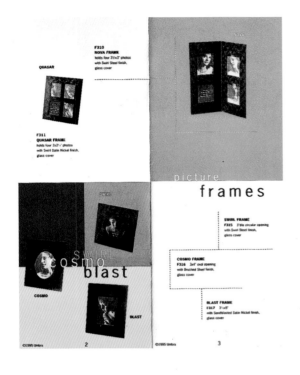

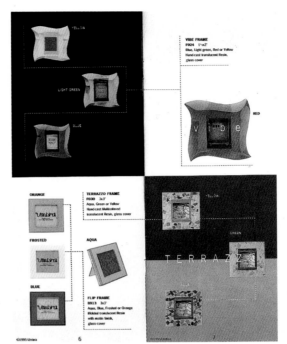

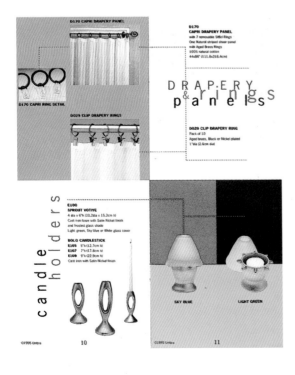

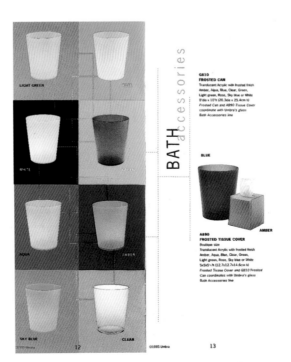

雑貨メーカー　製品案内
**Housewares Manufacturer
Supplementary Product Catalogue**
USA / Canada　1995

CD, AD, D : **Claudia Neri**

P : **Chris Barnes**

DF : **Teikna**

CL : **Umbra Ltd.**

SIZE : **280 × 108mm**

家具販売会社　プロモーション
Furniture Distributor
Promotional Direct Mail
Japan　1996

CD, AD, D : **Makoto Orisaki**

P : **Kuni Shinohara**

DF : **Makoto Orisaki Design**

CL : **E & Y Co., Ltd.**

SIZE : **225 × 210mm / 210 × 210mm**

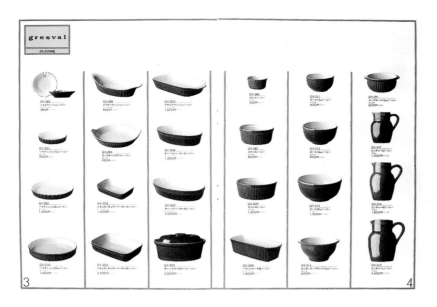

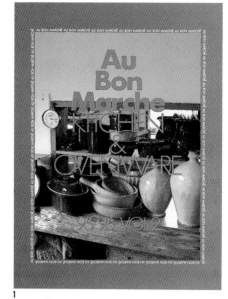

3　4　1

5　6

テーブルウェアーメーカー　製品案内
Tableware Manufacturer
Product Catalogues
Japan　1995

CD. AD. D : Takashi Yamada

D : Manabi Sasaki（2）

P : Masanori Kashino

DF : Work Shop Inc.

CL : Kinto & Corporation

SIZE : 297 × 210mm

LIRICA　EPICA　MOLINO　CASA

SINCERE　HERBE　PRADOR

PILIER PLANTER　FLEUR　TORRE

3　4

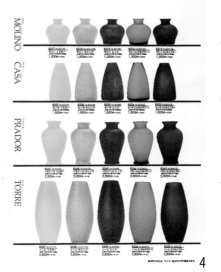

2

タイルメーカー　製品案内
Tile Manufacturer　Product Brochure
USA　1991

CD, AD, D : Jose Serrano
P : Carl Vanderschuit / Steve Simpson
I : Nancy Stahl / Tracy Sabin
DF : Mires Design, Inc.
CL : Deleo Clay Tile Co.
SIZE : 277×216mm

Page 95
手帳／アルバム販売会社　製品案内
Journal / Album Manufacturer
Retailor Catalogue
USA　1996

CD, AD, D : Mark J. Leroy
P : Carey Hendricks Photography
I, CW : Pamela Barsky
DF : Mark Designs
CL : Pamela Barsky Wholesale
SIZE : 254×95mm

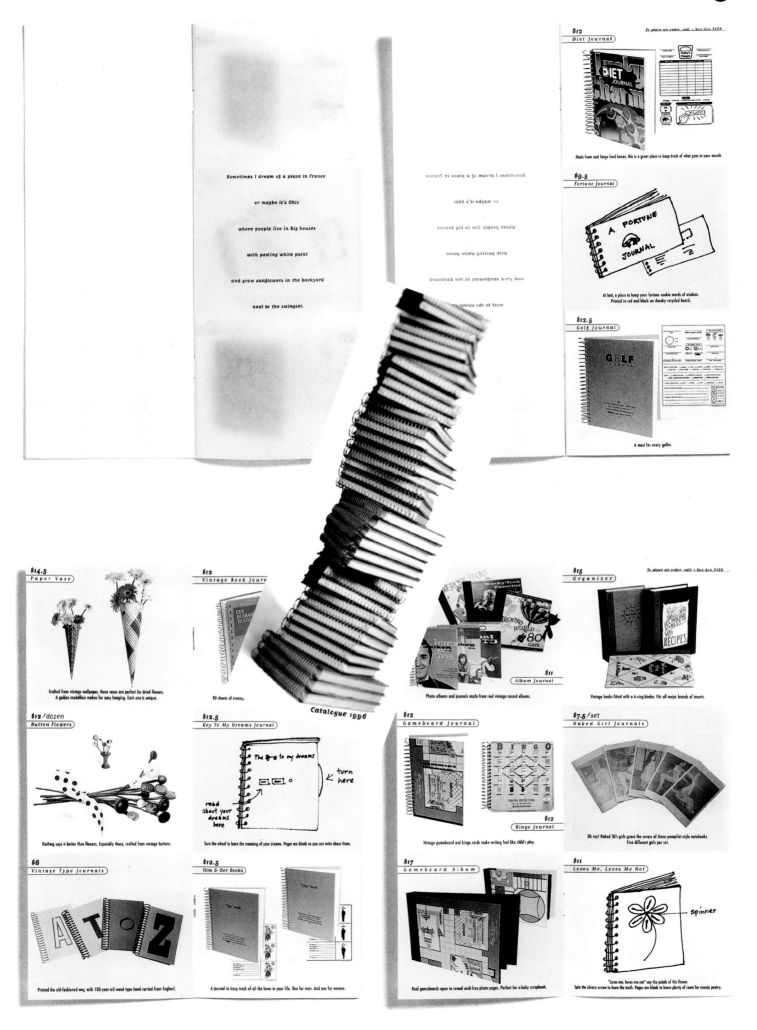

Sometimes I dream of a place in France

or maybe it's Ohio

where people live in big houses

with peeling white paint

and grow sunflowers in the backyard

next to the swingset.

Catalogue 1996

To place an order, call: 1.800.600.3458

$12
Diet Journal

Made from real binge food boxes, this is a great place to keep track of what goes in your mouth.

$9.5
Fortune Journal

A FORTUNE JOURNAL

At last, a place to keep your fortune cookie words of wisdom.
Printed in red and black on chunky recycled board.

$12.5
Golf Journal

GOLF

A must for every golfer.

$14.5
Paper Vase

Crafted from vintage wallpaper, these vases are perfect for dried flowers.
A golden medallion makes for easy hanging. Each one is unique.

$12
Vintage Book Journal

90 sheets of creamy .

$11
Album Journal

Photo albums and journals made from real vintage record albums.

To place an order, call: 1.800.600.3458

$15
Organizer

RECIPES

Vintage books fitted with a 6-ring binder. Fits all major brands of inserts.

$12/dozen
Button Flowers

Nothing says it better than flowers. Especially these, crafted from vintage buttons.

$12.5
Key To My Dreams Journal

The key to my dreams

turn here

read about your dreams here

Turn the wheel to learn the meaning of your dreams. Pages are blank so you can write about them.

$12
Gameboard Journal

BINGO

$12
Bingo Journal

Vintage gameboard and bingo cards make writing feel like child's play.

$7.5/set
Naked Girl Journals

Oh my! Naked 50's girls grace the covers of these pamphlet-style notebooks.
Five different girls per set.

$6
Vintage Type Journals

A T O Z

Printed the old-fashioned way, with 100-year-old wood type hand-carried from England.

$12.5
Him & Her Books

"Him" book

A journal to keep track of all the loves in your life. One for men. And one for women.

$17
Gameboard Album

Real gameboards open to reveal acid-free photo pages. Perfect for a baby scrapbook.

$11
Loves Me, Loves Me Not

spinner

"Loves me, loves me not" say the petals of this flower.
Spin the silvery arrow to learn the truth. Pages are blank to leave plenty of room for moody poetry.

フローリングメーカー　製品案内
Flooring Manufacturer　Product Brochures
UK　1993

CD : **Jeff Kindleysides**

D : **Matthew Fawell**

DF : **Checkland Kindleysides**

CW, CL : **The Amtico Co., Ltd.**

SIZE : **279 × 209mm**

From the distinctive

to the inimitable...

With its great versatility and design potential, Amtico lends itself to creative interpretation and we are delighted to help our customers realise their 'dream' floors. One such floor belongs to Sarah George.

Moving from an old cottage in the country to a modern town house, she had sacrificed a cherished antique bath and cosy bathroom for a featureless, internal room lined out in grey and white tiles. She began to dream up a scheme centred on the sea, incorporating a specially commissioned clinker-built boat-bath and an abstract seascape floor design.

Venturing into the Amtico Studio one morning, she was immediately impressed both by the product range and by the enthusiastic reception she got from the staff. 'I begin to understand what the company was all about that day: dynamic, enthusiastic, a make-it-happen company!' she recalls.

By utilising the Amtico Design Service, she was able to translate her initial ideas into distinctive reality. She chose products from the marble and metallic collections.

Sarah George has continued to develop the seascape theme since the floor went down. The ceiling is now a dual-level design in bird's eye maple. Inset around one of the ceiling downlights, is another starfish in Amtico's Celestial metallic burgundy. 'The product is so inspiring that I would like to put it to many other uses,' she says. 'Working with the company was an incredible experience. Seeing the floor down for the first time was a very exciting moment, one I'll long remember; one we celebrated!'

A TRULY VERSATILE MATERIAL, THE SCOPE OF WHICH IS UNLIMITED - A CREATIVE MIND CAN REALISE THE TRUE DESIGN POTENTIAL OF AMTICO.

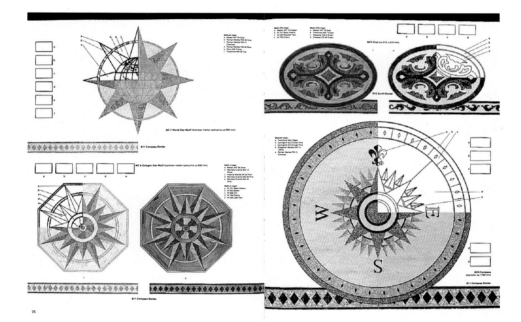

26

On l'a appelée la boutique la plus "in" d'Europe : la Boutique Destroy de John Richmond à Covent Garden, à Londres, possède un revêtement de sol Amtico "metallic pewter" (étain métallique), qui contraste vivement avec la moquette violette qui l'entoure et complète la juxtaposition frappante d'autres matériaux : briques sablées jouxtant l'acier inoxydable et aluminium poli, le xylorex.

David Fern, du cabinet de concepteurs The Fern Green Partnership, déclare : "Seuls les revêtements de sol Amtico nous ont offert la souplesse dont nous avions besoin pour donner libre cours à notre imagination. Nous n'avons rien vu d'autre qui permette une telle liberté d'expression."

Le chic industriel

Contrastes frappants et priorité aux considérations pratiques.

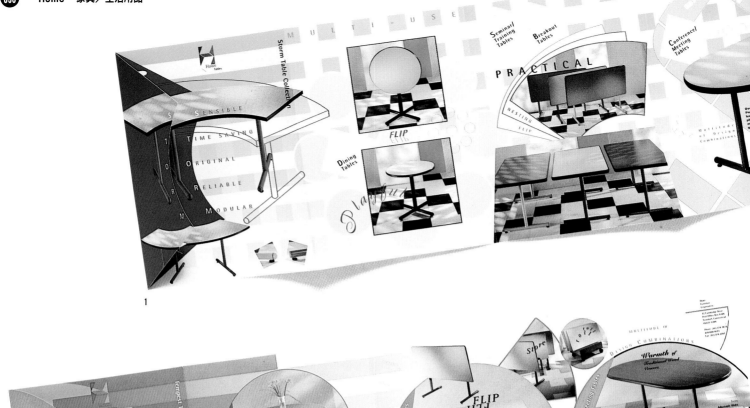

1

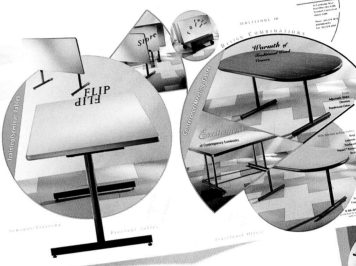

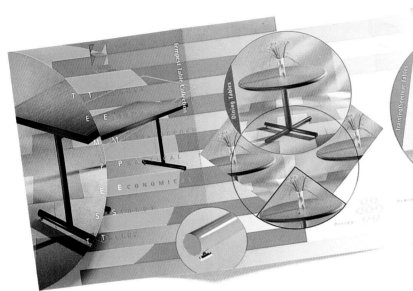

2

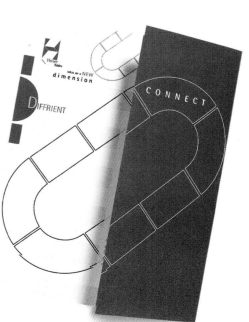

3

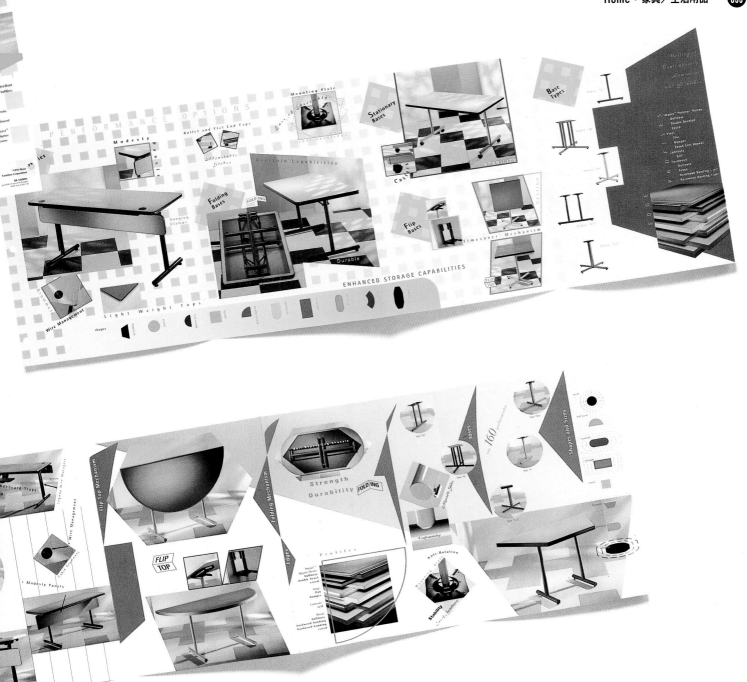

THE SURREY INSTITUTE OF ART & DESIGN

1. 家具メーカー　製品案内
Furniture Manufacturer
Product Brochure
USA　1995

CD : **Nancy Skolos**

AD, D : **E. Lokelani Lum-King**

D : **Spencer Ladd**

P : **Thomas Wedell**

DF : **Skolos / Wedell**

CL : **Home Furniture Corporation**

SIZE : **280 × 215mm**

2. 家具メーカー　製品案内
Furniture Manufacturer
Product Brochure
USA　1995

CD, D : **Nancy Skolos**

D : **Spencer Ladd**

P : **Thomas Wedell**

DF : **Skolos / Wedell**

CL : **Home Furniture Corporation**

SIZE : **280 × 215mm**

3. 家具メーカー　製品案内
Furniture Manufacturer
Product Brochures
USA　1995

CD, D : **Nancy Skolos**

P : **Thomas Wedell**

DF : **Skolos / Wedell**

CL : **Home Furniture Corporation**

SIZE : **280 × 215mm**

家具メーカー　製品案内
Furniture Manufacturer　Product Brochures
Italy　1996

CD：Barbara Cuniberti

AD, D：Carolyn O'connell

P：Luca Castelli

CW：Roberto Grandi

DF：Kuni Graphic Design Company

CL："Dreamspace" Modular S.R.L.

SIZE：285 × 230mm

L'accostamento di piani diversi, dotati di una geometria nuova, sorprendente, aggregati a colonne che li sostengono, assicura una variabilità compositiva rapida e sempre nuova. Tanti accessori per completare la facilità d'uso. Il programma comprende librerie, anche montate su ruote per spostarle secondo le diverse necessità.

The combination of different tops, endowed with a new, surprising geometry, joined by supporting columns, ensures numberless quick and easy solutions. Many accessories allow for easier utilization. The programme includes bookcases, mounted also on casters in order to move them according to need.

L'assemblage des divers plateaux, dotés d'une géométrie nouvelle, surprenante, rattachés à des colonnes qui les soutiennent, assure une variété de composition rapide et toujours renouvelée. De nombreux accessoires assurent un complément de confort. Le programme comprend des rangements montés éventuellement sur roues pour les déplacer selon les nécessités.

Die Zusammenstellung verschiedener geometrischer Flächen mittels tragender Säulen ermöglicht im Handumdrehen immer neue, variable Kompositionen. Viele Zubehörteile, wie auch Büroschränke auf Rollen, die ein Verrücken je nach Bedarf gestatten, machen das Programm benützerfreundlich.

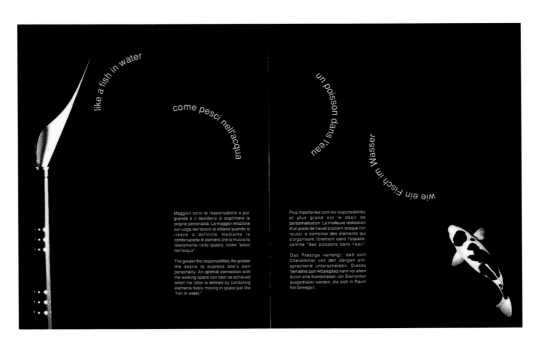

like a fish in water

come pesci nell'acqua

un poisson dans l'eau

wie ein Fisch im Wasser

Maggiori sono le responsabilità e più grande è il desiderio di esprimere le proprie personalità. La maggior relazione sul luogo del lavoro si ottiene quando si riesce a definirlo mediante la combinazione di elementi che si muovono liberamente nello spazio, come "pesci nell'acqua".

The greater the responsibilities the greater the desire to express one's own personality. An optimal connection with the working space can best be achieved when the latter is defined by combining elements freely moving in space just like "fish in water."

Plus importantes sont les responsabilités et plus grand est le désir de personnalisation. La meilleure réalisation d'un poste de travail s'obtient lorsque l'on réussit à combiner des éléments qui s'organisent librement dans l'espace, comme "des poissons dans l'eau".

Das Prestige verlangt, daß sich Chefzimmer von den übrigen entsprechend unterscheiden. Dieses Verhältnis zum Arbeitsplatz kann vor allem durch eine Kombination von Elementen ausgedrückt werden, die sich in Raum frei bewegen.

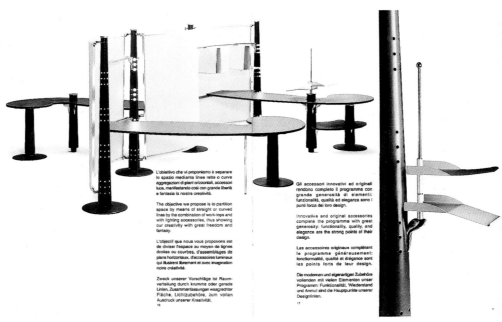

L'obiettivo che vi proponiamo è separare lo spazio mediante linee rette o curve, aggregazioni di piani orizzontali, accessori luce, manifestando così con grande libertà e fantasia la nostra creatività.

The objective we propose is to partition space by means of straight or curved lines by the combination of work-tops and with lighting accessories, thus showing our creativity with great freedom and fantasy.

L'objectif que nous vous proposons est de diviser l'espace au moyen de lignes droites ou courbes, d'assemblages de plans horizontaux, d'accessoires lumineux qui illustrent librement et avec imagination notre créativité.

Zweck unserer Vorschläge ist Raumverteilung durch krumme oder gerade Linien, Zusammenfassungen waagrechter Fläche, Lichtzubehöre, zum vollen Ausdruck unserer Kreativität.

Gli accessori innovativi ed originali rendono completo il programma con grande generosità di elementi: funzionalità, qualità ed eleganza sono i punti forza del loro design.

Innovative and original accessories complete the programme with great generosity: functionality, quality, and elegance are the strong points of their design.

Les accessoires originaux complètent le programme généreusement: fonctionnalité, qualité et élégance sont les points forts de leur design.

Die modernen und eigenartigen Zubehöre vollenden mit vielen Elementen unser Programm: Funktionalität, Wiederstand und Anmut sind die Hauptpunkte unserer Designlinien.

1

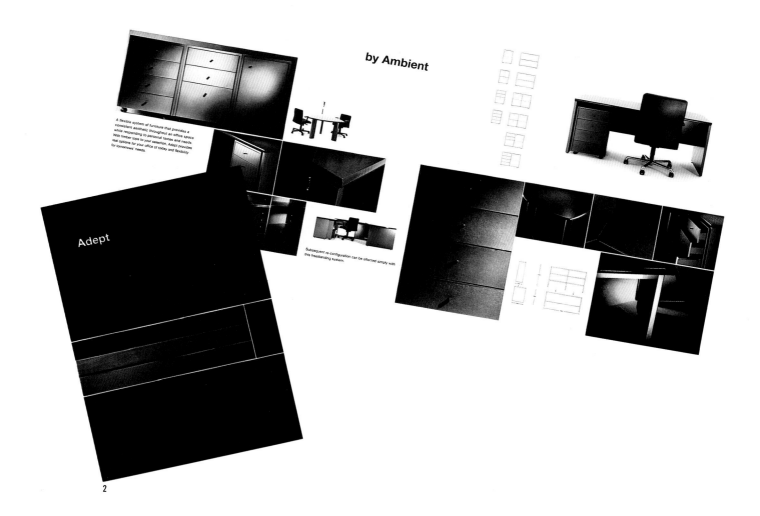

2

1. 家具メーカー　製品案内　**Furniture Manufacturer　Product Brochure**　Australia　1996
CD : **Fabio Ongarato** AD : **Ronnen Goren** D : **Belle Sambevska / Tim Richardson** P : **Jack Sarafian** DF : **Fabio Ongarato Design** CL : **Ambient Contract Interiors Pty Ltd.** SIZE : **297 × 210mm**

2. 家具メーカー　製品案内　**Furniture Manufacturer　Product Catalogue**　Australia　1995
CD, AD, D : **Fabio Ongarato** P : **Philip Korczynski** DF : **Fabio Ongarato Design** CL : **Ambient Contract Interiors Pty Ltd.** SIZE : **297 × 210mm**

食品メーカー
プロモーション用ゲームポスター
Food Producer　Game Poster
USA　1992

CD, AD, D : Sergio Steuer

CD : Donald Burg

I : Dan Brawner

DF : Porter / Novelli

CL : Kellogg Company

SIZE : 305 × 228mm

ワインメーカー　製品案内
Winery　Promotional Brochure
USA　1995

D : **Jeffrey Caldewey**

DF : **Caldewey Design**

CL : **Boisset USA**

SIZE : **110 × 215mm**

ワインメーカー　プロモーション
Winery　Promotional Brochure
Australia　1994

CD, D : **Ben Phillips**

AD : **Rick Lambert**

I : **Kathy Morgan**

CW : **Tony Lord**

DF : **Rick Lambert Design**

CL : **Chapman's Creek Vineyard**

SIZE : **210 × 100mm**

Rhine Riesling

1993

The wine was made from Frankland River fruit, a rapidly emerging region for this variety, as James Halliday has noted.

Vivacious straw green colour. Fresh, crisp and clean aroma with green apple overtones. Fresh and attractive flavour with light floral touches and clean fruit. The finish is crisp and mouthwatering. A perfect aperitif wine for drinking anytime. Goes well with cold chicken, fresh prawns, fish dishes, and fresh fruit desserts. It is a very versatile wine.

Chardonnay

1993

This Margaret River wine has been made with a nod to French white burgundy. Straw colour. Clean and clear aroma, bordering on flinty fresh. Hints of lychee and toasty oak. Fresh and flinty dry flavour, with a touch of butterscotch, elegant, and oak adding complexity.

Charming on its own. Complements all seafoods, especially oysters, creamy pasta, veal, and most Chinese dishes.

Shiraz

1993

From a very old vineyard just to the north of Margaret River. The age of the vine is reflected in the intensity of aroma and flavour. Rich ruby purple. Warm and generous aroma, bags of black pepper and oaky vanillan touches.

Firm and dry flavour, crushed black peppercorns. Great personality and will improve in bottle. Serve with any red meat dish and at barbies.

Cabernet Sauvignon

1993

A lighter style of red, but with regional characters. Deep purple red. Aroma displays regional blackcurrant scents, nice fruit, a touch of white pepper from the oak. Nicely soft and rounded flavour, quite dry, with a light grip coming at the finish from oak.

A good drinking red to go with pasta dishes with a tomato-based sauce, chicken, pork, veal, but sits easily with any dish calling for a dry red wine. For drinking now.

Tawny Port

Tony Lord is a great port man, and, found this lovely old tawny in the Barossa Valley. Unique as it is made only from Touriga, the top variety for port in Portugal. Rich tawny gold. Smooth velvet aroma, with a rancio character, and touches of dried sultanas. Smooth and elegant flavour, delicately sweet, slips down a treat. Outstanding value for money.

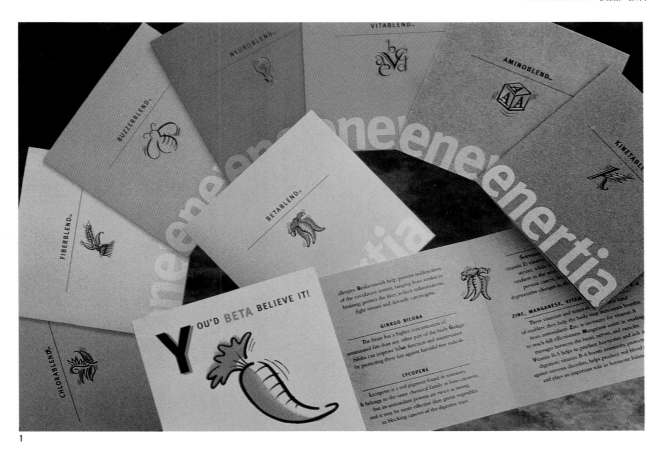

1

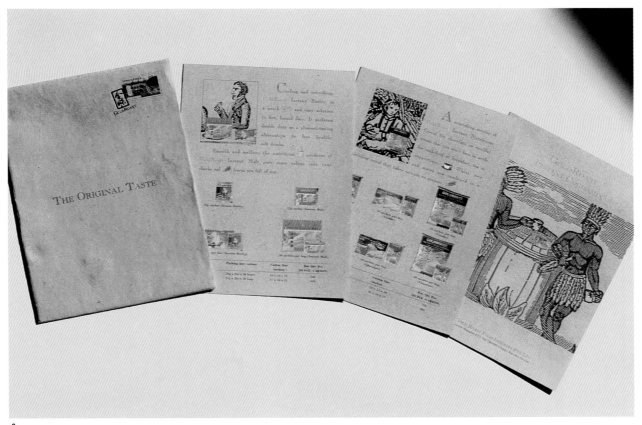

2

1. 飲料メーカー　製品案内　Juice Producer　Product Brochures　USA　1995
AD, D：Jack Anderson　D：Lisa Cerveny / Suzanne Haddon　I：Mits Katayama　CW：Suky Hutton　DF：Hornall Anderson Design Works, Inc.　CL：Jamba Juice　SIZE：101×101mm

2. 飲料メーカー　製品案内　Beverage Maker　Product Brochures　Singapore　1994
CD, AD：Coreen Aw　D, I：Eileen Koh　P：Mun's Studio　CW：Edwin Francis　DF：Sixteen-O-Two Advertising N' Design　CL：Gold Roast Food Industry Pte Ltd.　SIZE：292×210mm

ワイン／食品販売会社　商品案内
Wine / Food Retailer
Direct Mail Catalogue
USA　1995

D : **Jeffrey Caldewey**

DF : **Caldewey Design**

CL : **Bounty Hunter Rarewine & Provisions**

SIZE : **95 × 215mm**

PAHLMEYER, *Napa Valley*
Raiders of the lost vines

Jayson Pahlmeyer's entree into the wine business has all the elements of a Spielberg film: great action, foreign intrigue, sleight of hand. Action!

Opening Scene: Jayson and his partner discovered a hillside property in the Coombsville region of Napa in 1975. They promptly embarked on a three-year program **to acquire the best clones for a classic Bordeaux blend.** Easier said than done.

Scene Two: Jayson shipped budwood garnered from the most prestigious vineyards of Bordeaux to Canada. He would receive word of each shipment's arrival, fly from San Francisco to Buffalo (have some chicken wings at the Anchor Bar—the honest-to-goodness birthplace of buffalo chicken wings), then rent a van to transport the contraband plant material across the border at Niagara Falls. (Slowly I turned...) Finally, a major overland carrier was engaged to shepherd the goods to Napa.

16

The Plot Thickens... Everything was "jake" until the final shipment was received in Canada. Jayson's partner was dispatched to import the goods, but this time, rented a sedan instead of a van. He drove the route eight times before a customs agent became curious. (I hate it when that happens... you never want to make the Feds curious...)

The Exciting Conclusion: Rumor has it that somehow, just enough California budwood was sitting in storage when the Feds arrived to reclaim the smuggled "French" goods. How is that for intrigue? Uncork a bottle of the Oscar-caliber Pahlmeyer Red Table Wine, call a friend and slip in the "Disclosure" video. (Yet another way to become excited about Pahlmeyer wine.) Skip the popcorn.

"Drink now or cellar — it only gets better! A consistent award winner."

The Wines—

#410 Pahlmeyer Red Table Wine (Bordeaux Blend) 1992: Helen Turley, (hot-hot-hot) winemaker. Well-crafted wine. Cassis and oak, balanced tannins. Rich and deliciously complex.
$33.00/btl.　$29.70 btl./case of 12

#412 Jayson Red Table Wine 1992: Rich Merlot-based blend with berry, spice and leather notes. Veal chops are a must.
$20.00/btl.　$18.00 btl./case of 12

#411 Pahlmeyer Chardonnay 1993: Of "Disclosure" fame...the very wine that brought Demi to her knees. Unfined and unfiltered — in the raw. Ripe apple fruit, vanilla spice and sweet oak, hang on for a very long finish!　$33.00/btl.　2-btl. limit. (Trust me, you can't handle any more.)

"As a Cadillac lover, I know each model like I know wine Vintages."

Phone Orders 1-800-943-9463　♠　Fax Orders 1-707-257-2202

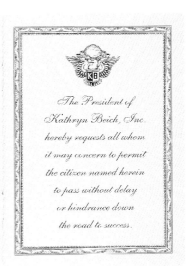

食品メーカー　営業推進ガイド
Food Producer
Pocket Guide for Sales People
USA　1993

CD, AD, D : **Bruce Edwards**

CW : **Julie Carpenter**

DF : **Rapp Collins Communications**

CL : **Kathryn Beich, Inc.**
　　 (fundraising division of Nestle)

SIZE : **127 × 87mm**

Earn the annual grand prize based on the total number of miles you accumulate.

If, among all consultants, you accumulate the greatest number of miles over the course of the program, you will earn the grand prize. To win the grand prize, however, your net sales for school year '93-'94 must be greater than your net sales from the previous year. If the first place mileage earner does not meet the qualifier, the grand prize will be awarded to the consultant with next highest mileage total who does meet the qualification. For a description of the grand prize, please see page 20 in this booklet.

Monthly Prizes

2-PIECE SAMSONITE LUGGAGE SET
Get ready to take off with this stylish luggage. Set includes a spacious boarding bag and a deluxe garment bag with plenty of room to keep all of your clothes looking fresh and wrinkle free. Available in black, teal, or blue.

12　　13

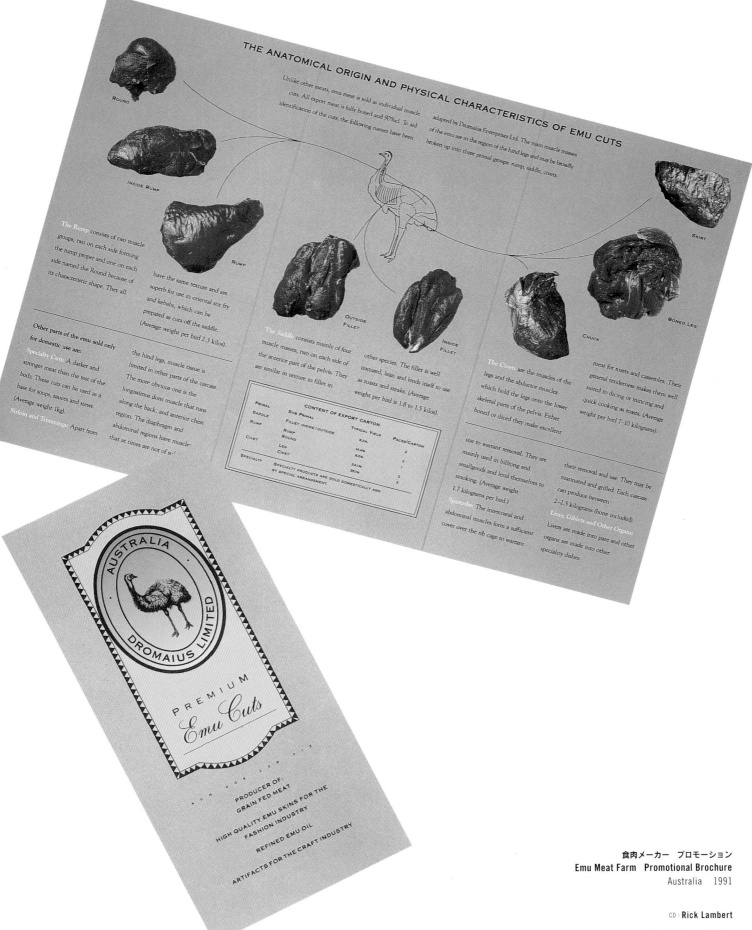

食肉メーカー　プロモーション
Emu Meat Farm　Promotional Brochure
Australia　1991

CD : Rick Lambert
CD, AD, D, I : Ben Phillips
DF : Rick Lambert Design
CW, CL : Dromaius Limited
SIZE : 297 × 140mm

Mondose - Eurofood's favourite chocolates

Jeff de Bruges - a European approach to flavour

Jeff de Bruges - Une nouvelle approche du bon goût

Jeff de Bruges - Een smaakvolle aanval op Europa

Jeff de Bruges - Ein süsser Frontal auf Europa

Artal - growing with the food industry, worldwide

Artal - Une croissance internationale liée à l'industrie alimentaire

Artal - Het vooruitstrekker in de internationale voedingsindustrie

CRÉATEUR DE CHOCOLATS
FRAIS DEPUIS 1857

THE TIN COLLECTION

LIQUEUR COLLECTION

neuhaus

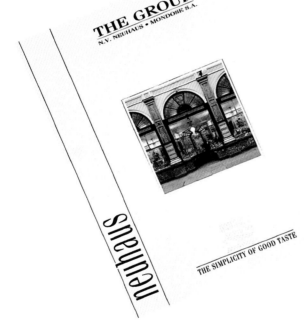

THE GROUP
N.V. NEUHAUS · MONDOSE S.A.

neuhaus

THE SIMPLICITY OF GOOD TASTE

neuhaus

BARS & TABLETS

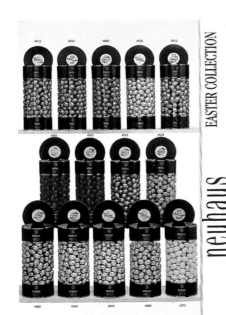

neuhaus

EASTER COLLECTION

neuhaus

THE OPERA COLLECTION

洋菓子メーカー　製品案内
Confectioner   Product Brochure

Japan   1996

CL : **Nihon Neuhaus Co., Ltd.**

SIZE : **297 × 210mm**

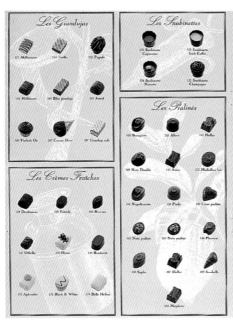

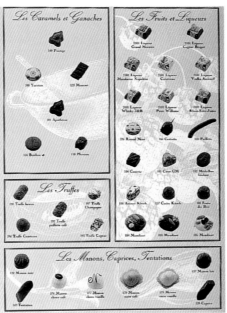

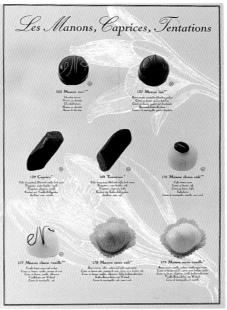

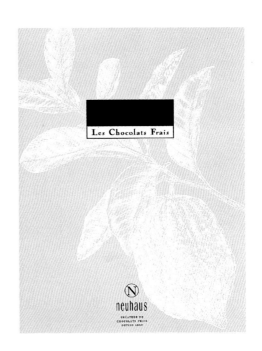

Les Chocolats Frais

neuhaus

洋菓子メーカー　製品案内
Confectioner Product Brochure
Japan 1996

CL : Nihon Neuhaus Co., Ltd.

SIZE : 297 × 210mm

グルメフードクラブ　プロモーション
Gourmet Food Club　Promotional Brochure
Hong Kong　1993

CD : **Kan Tai-keung**

AD. D : **Freeman Lau Siu Hong / Eddy Yu Chi Kong**

D : **Janny Lee Yin Wa**

P : **C. K. Wong / Idea Vision**

DF : **Kan Tai-keung Design & Associates Ltd.**

CL : **Membership Etc Ltd.**

SIZE : **265 × 265mm**

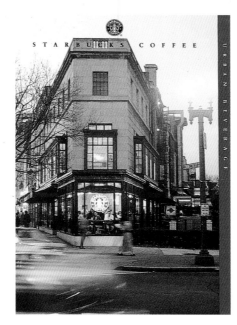

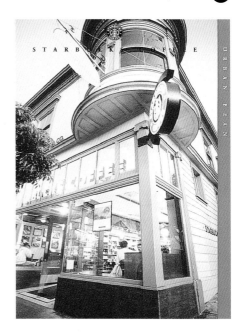

コーヒーメーカー　プロモーション
Coffee Company　Promotional Materials
USA　1995

AD, D : **Jack Anderson**

D : **Julie Lock / Julie Keenan /**

Jenny Woyvodich

P : **Jim Fagiolo**

I : **Julia LaPine**

DF : **Hornall Anderson Design Works, Inc.**

CW, CL : **Starbucks Coffee Company**

SIZE : **305 × 229mm**

*O*ur truffles are our most elegant chocolate pieces. Each is made with pure fresh cream, in the classic European tradition, then crafted into exquisite swirls. They're available in five varieties: Milk Chocolate, Dark Chocolate, Mocha, Mint, and smooth Irish Cream. Each is equally distinctive as a gift or as a dessert.

*E*ach glittering, foil-wrapped Liqueur Cream consists of a molded chocolate shell. Inside each shell lies a delightful surprise: a smooth cream filling blended with a generous measure of premium spirits: Amaretto, Orange Liqueur, Coffee Liqueur, Creme De Menthe, Bourbon, Rum, or Irish Cream. Nothing else captures the holiday spirit so well.

Assorted Truffles			Mint Truffle		
1 lb.	TRF	$14.50	1 lb.	MTRF	$14.50
2 lbs.	TRF2	$26.50	2 lbs.	MTRF2	$26.50
(Milk, Dark, Mocha)					
Irish Cream Truffle					
1 lb.	ICTRF*	$14.50			
2 lbs.	ICTRF2*	$26.50			

Liqueur Cream Assortment		
1 lb.	LIQ*	$14.50
2 lbs.	LIQ2*	$26.50
3 lbs.	LIQ3*	$38.50
5 lbs.	LIQ5*	$62.50

Please see the important notice on page 4 for restrictions regarding the shipment of Liqueur Creams.

Our Dime Truffles (inset) a beautiful chocolate surprise. It's also the smoothest, creamiest truffle we've ever had. So it's a treat you'll want to try.

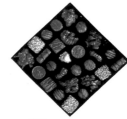

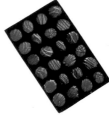

*I*f your special someone loves only Milk Chocolate, or has eyes only for Dark Chocolate, here's the ideal gift: an assortment of Nuts, Butter Creams, Caramels, and Solid Chocolates, all made with their favorite kind of rich Ethel M® Chocolate. In all, just the thing for people who know what they like, and who have friends who do, too.

*W*hat goes into a gift? If the gift is our Butter Cream Assortment, what goes in includes sun-ripened strawberries, tangy lemons, pure raspberries, Vermont maple sugar, costly Criollo cocoa beans, and grade AA creamery butter. Along with, of course, your very best wishes for the holiday season and the new year.

All Milk Chocolate			All Dark Chocolate		
1 lb.	MILK	$14.50	1 lb.	DARK	$14.50
2 lbs.	MILK2	$26.50	2 lbs.	DARK2	$26.50
3 lbs.	MILK3	$38.50	3 lbs.	DARK3	$38.50
5 lbs.	MILK5	$62.50	5 lbs.	DARK5	$62.50

All Milk Chocolate			*(Strawberry, Raspberry,*
1 lb.	BUT-MK	$14.50	*Chocolate, Butter-Rum, and*
2 lbs.	BUT-MK2	$26.50	*Maple Walnut Creams)*
All Dark Chocolate			*(Strawberry, Raspberry,*
1lb.	BUT-DK	$14.50	*Chocolate, Vanilla, and*
2 lbs.	BUT-DK2	$26.50	*Lemon Creams)*
Milk and Dark Chocolate			*(Assorted Butter Creams)*
1 lb.	BUT-MDK	$14.50	
2 lbs.	BUT-MDK2	$26.50	

When visions of strawberries dance through your head, our Strawberry Butter Cream is a dream come true.

DERBIES

$\mathcal{D}$erbies™ are double-sized, double decker Pecan Patties. So you get twice the pecans, twice the caramel, and twice the chocolate in every mouthwatering bite. We start with hand-sorted, hand-selected pecans and cover them in hot caramel. Then, we stack two of these pecan-caramel delights together, and cover the whole Pattie in smooth and delicious Milk Chocolate or Dark Chocolate. The result is a Pecan Pattie lover's dream come true. Derbies™ Double Decker Pecan Patties are available only from Ethel M Chocolates. They're available in assortments of Milk Chocolate, Dark Chocolate, or a mixture of both Milk and Dark.

Derbies™ All Milk
18 oz. DRB-MK $18.00 (2-9 oz. boxes)
Derbies™ All Dark
18 oz. DRB-DK $18.00 (2-9 oz. boxes)
Derbies™ Milk and Dark
18 oz. DRB-MDK $18.00 (2-9 oz. boxes)

Our popular Derbies™ Double Decker Pecan Patties feature twice the hearty pecans, twice the flowing caramel, and twice the rich chocolate for a doubly-good delight.

ETHEL M CHOCOLATE
IT'S BETTER TO GIVE™

ETHEL M is a registered trademark of Ethel M Chocolates, Inc.

洋菓子販売会社　通信販売用カタログ
**Confectionery Retailer
Mail Order Catalogue**
USA 1991

CD, AD, D : **José Serrano**

P : **Carl Vanderschuit**

DF : **Mires Design, Inc.**

CL : **Ethel M**

SIZE : **198 × 174mm**

DELUXE WITH LIQUEUR ASSORTMENT

DELUXE ASSORTMENT

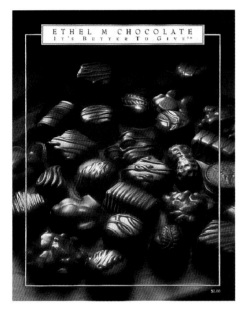

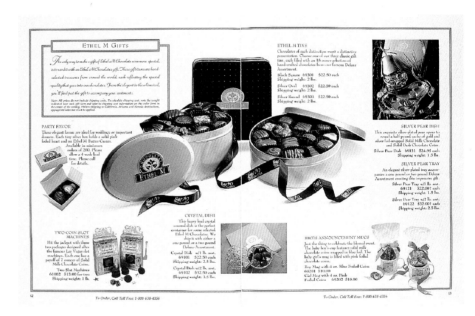

洋菓子販売会社　通信販売用カタログ
**Confectionery Retailer
Mail Order Catalogue**
USA　1991

CD, AD, D : **José Serrano**

P : **Carl Vanderschuit**

DF : **Mires Design, Inc.**

CL : **Ethel M**

SIZE : **238 × 178mm**

旅行代理店　ツアー案内
Travel Agency
Triathlete Training Spot Brochure
Germany　1995

CD : **Markus Friebe**

AD : **Andreas Klober**

D : **Andreas Wagner**

DF : **Convex Design Group Germany**

CL : **Top Fit-Trainingsreisen**

SIZE : **297 × 210mm**

旅行会社　ツアー案内
Travel Company　Youth Tour Pamphlet
Austria　1994

CD, AD, D, CW : **Peter Felder**

P, CW : **Heinz Rhomberg**

DF : **Felder Grafik Design**

CL : **Amt der Vorarlberger Landesregierung**
（Juqend-und Familienreferat）

SIZE : **190 × 110mm**

GO AWAY

& HAVE SOME FUN WITH YOUR BCS MEMBERSHIP CARD

ON HOLIDAYS WHEN YOU SHIP WITH US

宅配便会社　プロモーション
**Freight Forwarding Company
Service Brochures**
Singapore　1994

CD. AD : **Coreen AW**

D : **Gin Tee (1) / Edwin Franis (2)**

CW : **Magdalene Khoo (1) / Allan Tay (2)**

DF : **Sixteen-O-Two Advertising N' Design**

CL : **Breakbulk & Consolidation Services Pte Ltd.**

SIZE : **210 × 210mm**

GET OUT

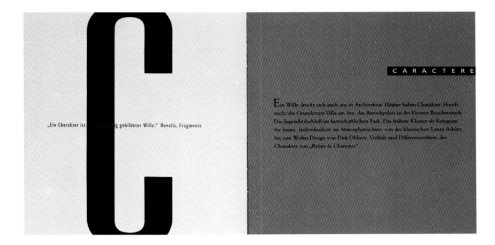

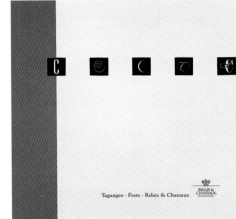

ホテル経営会社　プロモーション
Hotel Association　Promotional Brochure
Germany　1996

CD, AD, D, DF : **Marc Marahrens**

CW : **Hans Peter O. Breuer**

CL : **Relais de Chateaux**

SIZE : **165 × 165mm**

旅行代理店　ツアー案内
Travel Agency　Travel Service Brochure
Singapore　1994

CD, AD : **Coreen AW**

D, CW : **Edwin Francis**

I : **Eileen Koh**

DF : **Sixteen-O-Two Advertising N' Design**

CL : **American Express International, Inc. /
Travel Related Services**

SIZE : **297 × 210mm**

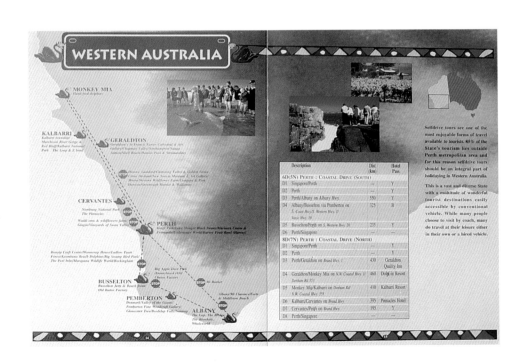

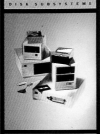

コンピューター周辺機器メーカー　製品案内
Workstations / Peripherals Manufacturer
Product Brochure
USA　1992

D, AD, D : **Mike Brower**

Carl Vanderschuit

F : **Mires Design, Inc.**

自動車メーカー　プロモーション
**Electric Car Manufacturer
Promotional Brochure**
France　1993

CD, AD, D : **Alain Lachartre**

CD, CW : **Philippe Blanchard**

I : **Francois Avril**

DF : **Vue Sur la Ville**

CL : **EDF**

SIZE : **269 × 169mm**

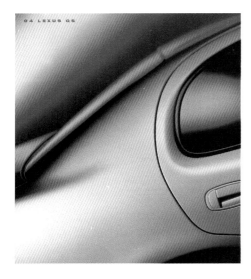

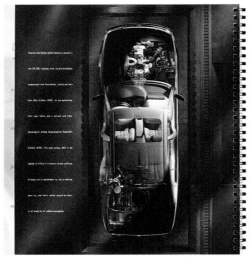

自動車メーカー　製品案内
Auto Manufacturer　Product Brochures
USA　1994

CD : **Tom Cordner**

AD : **Scott Bremner**

P : **Joe Baraban / Craig Cutleb /**

　Michael Ruppert / Vic Huber / RJ Muna

CW : **Neil Szigethy**

CL : **Lexus**

SIZE : **286 × 246mm**

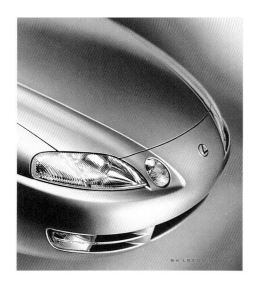

自動車メーカー　製品案内
Auto Manufacturer　Product Brochure
USA　1994

CD : Tom Cordner

AD : Scott Bremner

P : Joe Baraban / Craig Cutleb /

Michael Ruppert / Vic Huber / RJ Muna

CW : Neil Szigethy

CL : Lexus

SIZE : 313 × 253mm

Laguna

Vous êtes ici *chez vous*

自動車メーカー　製品案内
Auto Manufacturer　Product Brochure
France　1994

CD, AD, D : **Alain Lachartre**

CD, CW : **Philippe Blanchard**

CD : **Michel Armand**

P : **Keiichi Tahara / Michel Desmarteaux**

CL : **Renault**

SIZE : **296 × 234mm**

自動車メーカー　製品案内
Auto Manufacturer　Product Brochure
UK　1995

CD, D : **Richard Whitmore**

DF : **Checkland Kindleysides**

CL : **Toyota（GB）Limited**

SIZE : **240×298mm**

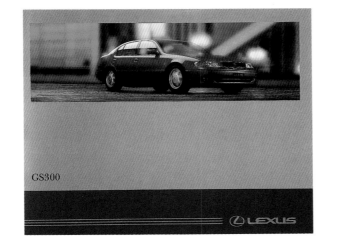

GS300

LEXUS

Performance with Responsibility

Exciting, exuberant, exotic... all these words describe the sporting character of the Lexus GS300. But despite its extrovert performance, this is not a car for exhibitionism but for those who can exercise power with discretion. Whisper-quiet and uncannily free of vibration, its road manners are impeccable. Despite its dynamic energy, the GS300 betrays no trace of immature bravado or brute force. Although endowed with all the strengths required for an executive express to attain high speeds - and then to haul it back to walking pace again in seconds - its potency is tempered by a keen sense of social and environmental responsibility.

Refined and responsive, the GS300's purpose-built, fuel-injected, Twin Cam 24-valve straight-six-cylinder engine produces a remarkable 209 bhp from just 3 litres. Put your foot down and it accelerates smoothly from 0-60 mph in 8.6 seconds, powering on to a potential 143 mph. Adopt a more refined style and it can return a creditable 36.2 mpg at a constant 56mph. Touch the brake pedal gently and its advanced computer-controlled high-performance anti-lock braking system (CCABS) will pull it to a straight line stop, whatever the weather, without hesitation. Alternately energetic or easy-going, the GS300 has a dual personality which changes to suit your mood.

Either way, when cruising lazily along the back-routes or moving more briskly down the motorway, the experience is always smoothly relaxed and civilised. The secret lies in the state-of-the-art, "thinking" transmission (ECT-i) pioneered in the LS400. This employs the electronic intelligence of two on-board computers to monitor events, memorise your driving style and anticipate your reactions, allowing the GS300 to sense your urgency when accelerating or slowing down, and thus match engine torque to the four-speed automatic transmission exactly. The result: silky-smooth shifts every time, even when changing gear under pressure.

6

A Concert Hall on Wheels

Behind the wheel of the Lexus GS300, the stage is set for quiet conversation or a full-scale symphony orchestra. Whatever your taste in music, modern or classical, jazz or rock, the GS300 offers the perfect mobile environment in which to enjoy your favourite music: on MW, LW, FM stereo radio, cassettes or multi-play compact discs. The vehicle's rigid structure and active sound and vibration insulation provide the ideal acoustic conditions for near perfect sound reproduction. Of course, the exclusive, fully-integrated in-car audio equipment installed is also of the very highest quality and specification, incorporating two separate amplifiers to provide an impressive 225 watts of total music power, transmitted through nine specially balanced speakers. A powerful, high-gain aerial automatically adjusts to the best position for the FM station selected. The radio unit also incorporates a network-following capability which monitors the strength of

transmissions to automatically select the strongest signal. The RDS radio incorporates features which allow it to receive traffic information broadcasts from the nearest station, so that even when you're playing tapes or CD, the sound may be interrupted briefly so that you can hear the bulletin. The Lexus GS300 is a car designed and built to transport its driver into the joys of musical appreciation. And as you and your passengers enjoy your private recital in this luxurious mobile concert hall, aware of the subtlest chords even in the noisiest traffic, you may reflect on the fact that the supplier of the fine Californian walnut veneers adorning the GS300's doors and fascia is the very same company famed for the deep lustrous finish of its grand pianos. Truly, the Lexus GS300 represents technology and craftsmanship in perfect harmony.

13

16

Lexus GS300 Specification

Performance Data

Acceleration*, 0-60mph	8.6 sec	
Maximum speed*	143 mph	
Fuel consumption**	Urban cycle	20.3 mpg	13.9l/100km
	Constant 56 mph	36.2 mpg	7.8l/100km
	Constant 75 mph	29.7 mpg	9.5l/100km
Towing capacity	Trailer with brake	1500 kg
	Trailer without brake	500 kg
Drag coefficient	Cd	0.31

* Manufacturer's figures
** Official figures. Fuel consumption depends upon many factors such as starting, motoring conditions. A particular car's fuel consumption may therefore vary from the figures shown.

Engine

Type	3.0 Litre In-Line 6 Twin Cam, 24-valve
Piston displacement	2997 cc
Bore and stroke	86.0mm x 86.0mm
Compression ratio	10.0 to 1
Max horsepower (DIN)	209 bhp at 5400 rpm
Max torque	205 lb.ft at 4800 rpm
Fuel system	Sequential multi-point injection
Fuel tank capacity	80 litres 17.6 gallons
Fuel type	Unleaded Only

Chassis

Suspension Front & Rear	4 wheel independent double wishbones, coil springs, gas-pressurised shock absorbers. Anti-dive and anti-squat geometry.
Brakes Front/Rear	296mm ventilated discs/307mm ventilated discs with ABS.
Transmission	4 speed automatic with intelligent electronically controlled transmission (ECT-i).
Steering	Rack and pinion, speed-sensitive variable power assistance.
Turning radius (tyres)	5.5m (kerb to kerb)
Tyres	225/55HR16 94V (to fitting spare)

Dimensions & Weight

Overall length	4850mm
Overall width	1795mm
Overall height	1425mm
Wheelbase	2780mm
Track Front	1505 mm
Track Rear	1515 mm
Kerb weight	1700 kg
Boot capacity VDA	0.401 m³
	14.3 ft³

17

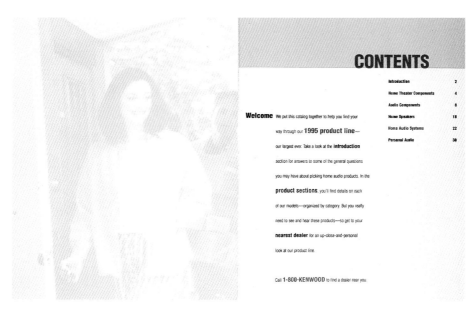

オーディオ機器メーカー　製品案内
**Audio Equipment Manufacturer
Product Brochure**
USA　1994

CD, AD : **Trina Nuovo**

D : **Carole Czapla**

P : **Ann Cutting**

CW : **Bob Drake**

DF : **White Plus**

CW, CL : **Kenwood USA Corporation**

SIZE : **279 × 216mm**

オーディオ機器メーカー　プレスキット
Audio Equipment Manufacturer　Press Kit
USA　1994

CD, AD : **Trina Nuovo**

D : **Victoria Berry**

P : **Henry Blackham**

DF : **White Plus**

CW, CL : **Kenwood USA Corporation**

SIZE : **305 × 228mm**

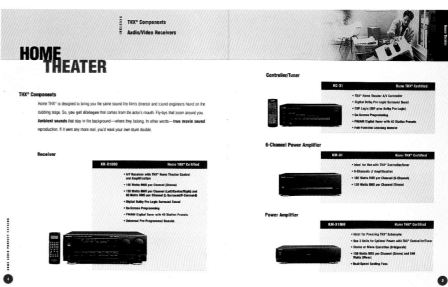

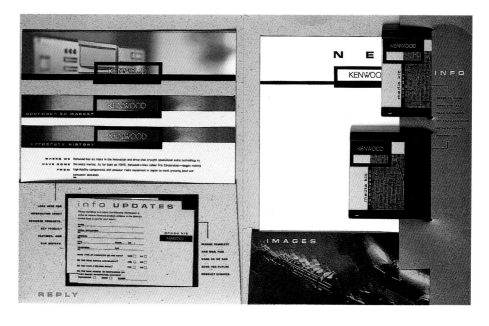

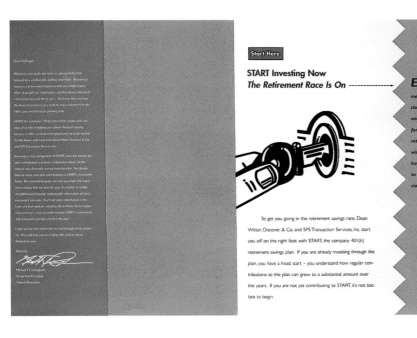

START Investing Now
The Retirement Race Is On ----------

Start Here

Every day, retirement is one day closer, and you have one less day to save for it. When you retire, will you be a winner? Will you have enough savings to assure a financially secure future?

To get you going in the retirement savings race, Dean Witter, Discover & Co. and SPS Transaction Services, Inc. start you off on the right foot with START, the company 401(k) retirement savings plan. If you are already investing through the plan, you have a head start – you understand how regular contributions to the plan can grow to a substantial amount over the years. If you are not yet contributing to START, it's not too late to begin.

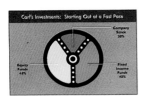

Questions

Your lifestyle will impact how much retirement will cost. For example, are you planning a retirement of world travel or days relaxing at home? Ask yourself the following questions:

yes   no

Do you plan to retire early, before age 65?
Are you planning to buy a retirement home?
Will you still have mortgage or rent payments on your primary residence?
Will you have college tuition to pay for your children?
Do you plan to travel a lot during retirement?
Will you need to purchase medical insurance?
Will you be supporting a spouse in retirement?

Of course, these are only some of the large expenses you could face during retirement. Still, if you answer "yes" to any of these questions, you'll need to factor those costs in with your retirement planning. There are several Dean Witter publications to help you find out how much you'll need to put aside for retirement. For example, enclosed with this brochure are copies of Financing Your Future (A Guide to Investing for Retirement) and an investment guide called Building Your Investment Portfolio (A Practical Guide to Asset Allocation). Once you've read these publications, feel free to speak with a Dean Witter Account Executive. The Account Executive can work with you to help you determine how much money you'll need in retirement and develop an investment strategy that is right for you.

Developing an Investment Strategy

Once you've given some thought to how much you'll need for a comfortable retirement, you can better determine which investment options are best suited to help you meet your goals. Of course, everyone wants their investments to earn as much income as possible, but there is an element of risk that you should consider when investing.

Balancing Risk and Reward

A race car driver understands the concept of risk versus reward. For example, a driver can't go full speed all the way through a race because that would increase the chances of getting into an accident. On the other hand, if the driver drove 10 miles an hour all the time, he or she would probably never crash – but would never win a race either. So the successful driver finds a balance.

The same is true for investing. Different investments have different levels of risk. Higher risk investments – such as stocks – can offer substantial returns over the long term, but there is also the chance that you might lose a portion of your investments if they perform poorly. On the other hand, if you deposit all your money in safe investments (like money market funds) you'll probably earn a steady income, but that income will be relatively small. In that case, you run the risk that your investments will not outpace inflation – meaning that you actually lose buying power over time (check the sidebar on page 6 for more inflation information). So, like the driver, you need to find a balance. Most investors find that balance by diversifying their portfolio in a variety of funds.

The performance history of START Plan funds can be found in each fund's prospectus.

A Look in the Winner's Circle

While only you can decide the best way to diversify your investments, let's take a look at the investment strategies of three goal-oriented investors. We'll start with Carl, who has just celebrated his 25th birthday. Carl has started the investment race on the right foot – he realizes the importance of beginning a consistent investment program at a young age. He also believes that there may be hurdles to overcome in the future (such as using his account to buy a first home) which could slow down his overall account growth. He wants to maximize his investment potential now, so he adopts an aggressive investment strategy for his START money. Here's Carl's investment mix.

any short-term downturns in the stockmarket since he has a long way to go until retirement. And, to balance his investments, he keeps 40% in fixed income funds.

Then there's Paula. She's in her 30's and believes the key to winning the retirement race is to diversify her investments. Paula likes variety – she strives to follow a steady course by contributing to START from each paycheck and chooses a combination of funds that carries a variety of risk levels. She monitors her investments, too, by studying her quarterly plan statements. This way, she can revise her investment regimen as needed. Here's how her investments shape up:

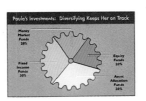

Carl's Investments: Starting Out at a Fast Pace

Company Stock 20%
Equity Funds 40%
Fixed Income Funds 40%

Paula's Investments: Diversifying Keeps Her on Track

Money Market Funds 20%
Fixed Income Funds 20%
Equity Funds 20%
Asset Allocation Funds 20%

Although Carl has a substantial amount of his investments in stock funds – 40% in equity funds and 20% in company common stock – he feels he can ride out

Paula has 20% of her money in money market funds, 20% in fixed income funds, 20% in asset allocation funds and 20% in equity funds.

ファイナンス会社　商品案内
Financial Company   Service Brochure
USA   1995

CD. AD. D : **Toni Schowalter**
I : **Chris Spollen**
DF : **Toni Schowalter Design**
CL : **Dean Witter**
SIZE : **305 × 223mm**

ローン会社　プロモーション
Loan Company　Promotional Kit
USA　1995

CD. AD. D. I : **John Sayles**

CW : **Allison Bishop**

DF : **Sayles Graphic Design**

CL : **Principal Residential Mortgage**

SIZE : **127 × 127 × 127mm**

(Photos by BLACK BOX STUDIOS, N.J.)

THE HUNTINGTON PERSONAL BANKERS WILL SOON BE GETTING A BRAND NEW

BABY*

*BRINGING AUTOMATED BANKING TO YOU!!!...

銀行　サービス案内
Bank
New Automation Promotional Brochure
USA　1993

CD, AD, D : **Eric Rickabaugh**
P : **Black Box**
CW : **Larry Sullivan**
DF : **Rickabaugh Graphics**
CL : **Huntington Banks**
SIZE : **165 × 159mm**

年金保険会社　サービス案内　Annuities Company　Promotional Brochure　USA　1994
AD, D : John Hornall　D : Lisa Cerveny / Suzanne Haddon　DF : Hornall Anderson Design Works, Inc.　CW, CL : GE / GNA Capital Assurance
SIZE : 260×273×66mm (Box) / 254×254mm (Brochure) / 56×56mm (Cube)

And your
employees may
be paying the price.

Introducing LifePoints – A smart

way to invest. A new way to communicate.

LifePoints.

But is anybody listening?

THE QUOTE ON THE COVER from the movie *"Cool Hand Luke,"* illustrates a challenge facing plan sponsors in the 1990s. With the growth of defined contribution plans, your employees are assuming more responsibility for retirement funding.

RUSSELL HOLDS EVIDENCE that this may be happening. Proprietary research shows traditional investment materials fail to reach or go unread by 70 percent of employees. We heard this loud and clear in focus groups and interviews

everybody is talking about saving for retirement.

THE INDUSTRY HAS RESPONDED with a menu of investment options, from the mundane to the exotic. And along with the investments comes a steady flow of reading materials, software, and videos. BUT IS IT WORKING? After all, investments are only as good as your employees' ability to use them. Likewise, communications is pointless if it leads to suboptimal choices.

with thousands of investors. YOUR EMPLOYEES NEED information, but they also need straight talk about investments, combined with sound guidance tailored to their LifePoint and tolerance for risk. LifePoints does that and more.

Frank Russell Company Financial Planning Behavior Research, 1994.

"What
we've got
here is a failure
to communicate."

Russell

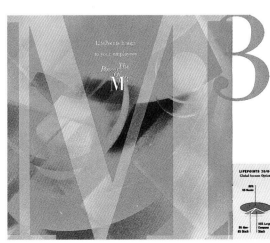

So why do we treat
them that way? People want

to be treated as individuals. That means providing investment choices and communications that speak to the uniqueness of their lives. The investment needs of the 50-year-old family man are distinct from the 35-year-old single mom, which are different still from someone who is 25 and single. The challenge has been delivering materials that meet tailored needs without breaking your budget. THE LIFEPOINTS MAP SEGMENTS EMPLOYEES INTO THREE BROAD CATEGORIES, HELPING THEM NARROW THEIR INVESTMENT FOCUS.

WHAT'S THE POWER OF M³? It's the power of diversifying investments called multi-asset, multi-style, multi-manager. The LifePoints strategies employ this tactic, which is the same one Russell recommends for the large pension plans of Fortune 500 companies. The strategies are balanced not just by asset class, but also by styles within each asset class. Additionally, Russell uses complementary money managers within each asset class, all of whom are specialists in a particular style.

FOR EXAMPLE, in the LifePoints 60/40 option, participant money would be managed by as many as 30 different money managers selected by Russell's exhaustive manager research process. Managers are continuously monitored and strategies are automatically rebalanced in line with their objectives. IN SHORT, this apparently simple strategy (in the eyes of your participants) would strongly resemble a portfolio assembled by a money manager with millions to invest. All Russell investments are built and managed using The Power of M³.

投資銀行　プロモーション
Investment Bank　Promotional Brochure
USA　1995

AD, D : **Jack Anderson**

D : **Lisa Cerveny / Suzanne Haddon**

DF : **Hornall Anderson Design Works, Inc.**

CW, CL : **Frank Russell Company**

SIZE : **190 × 190mm**

年金保険会社　サービス案内
Annuities Company　Promotional Materials
USA　1995

AD, D : **John Hornall**

D : **Lisa Cerveny / Suzanne Haddon**

DF : **Hornall Anderson Design Works, Inc.**

CW, CL : **GE / GNA Capital Assurance**

SIZE : **255 × 215mm**

1

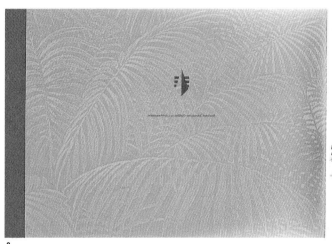

2

1. 不動産会社　商品案内
Real Estate / Development Company
Promotional Brochure
Australia　1995

CD, AD : **Rick Lambert**

D : **Mike Barker**

DF : **Rick Lambert Design**

CL : **International Assets**

SIZE : **285 × 221mm**

2. 不動産会社　商品案内
Real Estate / Development Company
Marketing Brochure
Australia　1994

CD, AD, D : **Rick Lambert**

D : **Ben Phillips**

CW : **Trevor Todd**

DF : **Rick Lambert Design**

CL : **International Assets**

SIZE : **230 × 304mm**

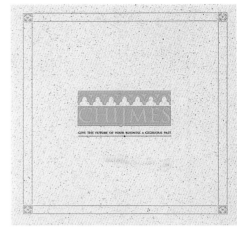

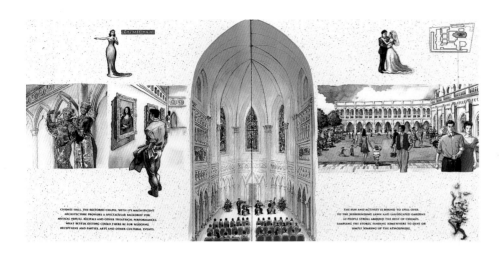

不動産会社　テナント募集案内
Property Development Company
Promotional Brochure
Singapore　1995

CD : **Allein Moore**

AD. D : **Ruth Scott**

I : **Owl Illustration**

CW : **Mike Mitchell**

CL : **Chijmes Investment Pte Ltd.**

SIZE : **270 × 270mm**

建設 / 不動産会社　不動産案内
Real Estate / Construction Company
Real Estate Guide
Brasil　1993

CD, CW : **Helena Deutsch Almeida Prado**

AD. D : **Luiz Henrique da Silva Cruz**

I : **Elson Issao**

DF : **L. H. Cruz Design & Fotografia**

CL : **Gafisa**

SIZE : **315 × 215mm**

1

2

1. ソフトウェア開発会社　製品案内　Software Development Company　Product Catalogue　USA　1995
AD, D : **John Hornall**　D : **Larry Anderson / Jenny Woyvodich / Debra Hampton / Eulah Sheffield**
P : **Darrell Peterson**　CW : **Jeff Fraga**　DF : **Hornall Anderson Design Works, Inc.**　CL : **Microsoft Corporation**　SIZE : **216 × 280mm**

2. デジタル画像ストック会社　商品案内　Digital Image Archiver　Direct Mail Promotion　USA　1995
AD, D : **Jack Anderson**　D : **John Anicker / David Bates**　CW : **Barry Briggs**　DF : **Hornall Anderson Design Works, Inc.**　CL : **Corbis**　SIZE : **255 × 180mm**

1. 情報管理会社　プロモーション　Information Storage & Retrieval Company　Promotional Brochure　USA　1995
AD, D : Jack Anderson　D : David Bates / Suzanne Haddon　CW : Barry Briggs　DF : Hornall Anderson Design Works, Inc.　CL : Intermation Corporation　SIZE : 286×196mm

2. 情報管理会社　プロモーション　Information Storage & Retrieval Company　Promotional Brochure　USA　1995
AD, D : Jack Anderson　D : David Bates / Suzanne Haddon　I : Eddie Yip　DF : Hornall Anderson Design Works, Inc.　CW, CL : Intermation Corporation　SIZE : 286×196mm

ソフトウェア開発会社　プロモーション
Software Development Company
Promotional Brochures
USA　1995

CD, AD, D, I, CW, DF : **Planet Design Company**

CL : **CE Software Incorporated**

SIZE : **290 × 189mm**

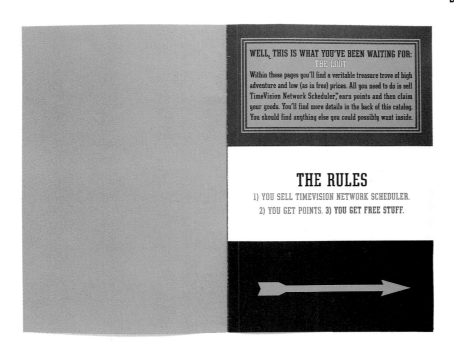

WELL, THIS IS WHAT YOU'VE BEEN WAITING FOR:
THE LOOT.

Within these pages you'll find a veritable treasure trove of high adventure and low (as in free) prices. All you need to do is sell TimeVision Network Scheduler,™ earn points and then claim your goods. You'll find more details in the back of this catalog. You should find anything else you could possibly want inside.

THE RULES

1) YOU SELL TIMEVISION NETWORK SCHEDULER.
2) YOU GET POINTS. 3) **YOU GET FREE STUFF.**

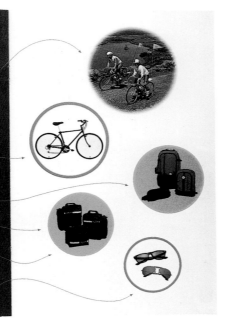

The VBT Bicycle Tour — Weekend: 11,500 Points/Five Day: 16,500 Points

It's said you can't run away from your problems. So why not try pedaling away? Few things let you escape the day-to-day routine as completely as a VBT bicycle tour. VBT offers the absolute finest in weekend and five day tours through some of the most beautiful areas in America. Each tour is carefully planned for beginner, intermediate and advanced level cyclists. Regardless of your skill level, you'll discover country roads leading to crystal-clear lakes, historic villages, romantic covered bridges, fields of wildflowers and panoramic views.

Friendly and knowledgeable VBT leaders provide you and a guest with information and support along every step of the way. And that's not all. While your days are spent outdoors, your nights are spent relaxing at only the coziest of country inns. Each has been selected for comfort, charm, cuisine and hospitality. Includes airfare and spending money. For more information, please call (800) 523-7638.

The Bianchi Strada — 1,625 Points

Whether you're looking to get around town or get out of town, the Bianchi Strada is the way to do it. Built with a full chrome-moly frame, the Strada features Shimano brakes and derailleurs and the GripShift Quick Shift system for easy operation. The Strada's hybrid design assures comfort by allowing you to ride in an upright position.

The Eagle Creek Endless Journey Backpack System — 1,375 Points

For long-haul adventure travel, it's hard to beat the Endless Journey. With 5,700 cubic inches of capacity, this 3-in-1 travel system features both a zip-off day pack and a zip-off waist pack for short trips. A horseshoe zipper provides access to the lower pack while an internal divider panel can be removed when needed to create an extra large main compartment. Available in Black.

The Lone Peak Mount Rainier P-850 Pannier — 850 Points

For the serious hiker, we offer Lone Peak's Mount Rainier pannier. This expedition-capacity pannier features six large external pockets which amount to 2,500 cubic inches of storage per pair. Compression straps provide stability no matter what the load. (This pannier requires a rear rack on your bicycle.) Available in Black.

The Lone Peak Atta Handlebar Pack — 485 Points

Designed to fit a wide variety of handlebars, the Atta carries 660 cubic inches worth of gear. An internal stash pocket and elastic loops secure small items while a weather-proof, clear map cover keeps documents dry and readable. Available in Black, Forest/Black, Blue/Black or Grey/Black.

The Ray-Ban Driving Series Sunglasses — 400 Points

The Wayfarer II and Outdoorsman sunglasses are part of the Ray-Ban Driving Series. With ChroMax Color Contrast Technology, they selectively filter light to make traffic signals, brake lights and signs appear brighter and easier to see. And on top of that, they're as cool as all get out. Styles: Wayfarer II (Mock Tortoise), Outdoorsman (Arista with black brow) or Outdoorsman II (for bigger faces).

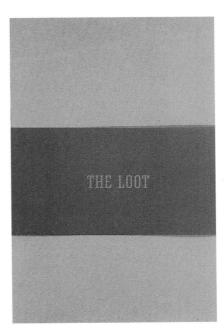

THE LOOT

The Weekend Shopping Adventure — 10,500 Points

This is the perfect trip for the person who doesn't have everything—but would like to try to get it. Your choice of shopping destinations are either New York, Chicago or San Francisco. Included in the package are airfare for two, one night's hotel, meal expenses and $300 dollars in cash. How you spend your money during the weekend is completely up to you. And fortunately, the same is true for how you spend your time. For more information please call (800) 523-7638.

The Boyt Mach II® Luggage Set — 4,150 Points

Although some say you can't take it with you, anyone with this five piece set of Boyt luggage might disagree. Boyt, a recognized industry leader, developed the Mach II line to stylishly withstand the rigors of travel in the 90s. After almost a century of experience, it's with confidence that they back each bag with a lifetime guarantee. The luggage in this set includes: the Walk-In Closet™ Garment Bag (42"x25"x4"), the Glider™ Vacationer (24"x18"x8"), the Attachable Latch Tote (12"x12"x5"), the Deluxe Expandable Carry-On (21"x13"x8-11"), and the Deluxe Shoulder Tote (16"x12"x9"). All bags are available in Black.

The Lands' End or Eddie Bauer® Gift Certificates — 1,500 Points

For the finest in casual clothing, it's hard to beat Lands' End and Eddie Bauer. All you need to do is choose which $300 gift certificate you'd prefer and then you're ready to shop.

The CE Software Multi-Sport Jacket — 750 Points

This three-in-one jacket features a heavyweight nylon outer shell with a hidden hood, a zip front and an especially attractive CE Software logo. The zip-in/zip-out inner jacket, which can be worn alone, is made of 100% polyester fleece liner. In bad weather, combine both jackets for extra protection. Available in Black/Violet/Aqua or Navy/Pine/Saddle. Please specify S, M, L, XL, XXL or XXXL.

Gift Certificate

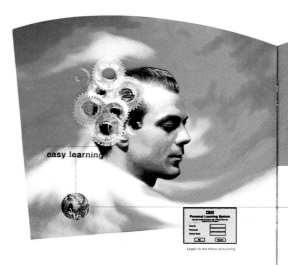

Dreams...

In an ideal world training and learning would happen in a relaxed environment, providing regular contacts with professionals or specialists.

Of course, what usually happens is that training sessions are inconveniently scheduled and located, forcing you to cram courses into an already busy schedule leaving you to catch up for the hours away from the job.

easy learning

...become reality...

The solution is to provide effective training where and when it's needed.

Now it's possible to deliver a variety of courses that call upon any and all media (sound, graphics, text, photo images and video) which are easy to develop, distribute and most importantly - instantly accessible.

...with IBM's
Personal Learning System

Logon to the future of learning

Integrate, Enhance & Develop...

Integrate material from various existing sources (e.g. computer based training (CBT), videos, slide shows, documentaries, printed product descriptions and presentations) into a single delivery platform.

Enhance and preserve existing material by making linear video interactive, adding tests, reference materials, subtitles and even audio dubbing.

Develop new courses with the easy to use PLS «mini» authoring tool.

Single point of access

...on an Open Platform.

Lessons can be based on Multimedia «chunks» derived from any or all of the following:
- the PLS authoring tool
- other authoring tools (e.g. ToolBook, IconAuthor, ...)
- programming languages (C, C++, ...)

multimedia

Learn at your own place...

Fewer schedules to coordinate. Less time away from the office. With PLS on a Local Area Network (LAN), separate PC or on a CD-ROM, simply take a course when it's convenient.

Instant access to courses offers an opportunity for significant savings on travel time and expenses. That makes you more productive. You're no longer bound by busy work schedules or the availability of trainers and their courses.

...and at your own pace...

Access courses at random or in a specific sequence. Go through material quickly or in as much detail as you like. Available on-line tools such as glossaries, references and pre-tests / post-tests provide knowledge assessments throughout the learning process. A complete range of topics can be available at your finger tips. All delivered in the language of your choice.

...but not on your own.

PLS won't leave you in isolation. With on-line messaging, bridges to E-mail and user comment tools, the expert and learner are easily put in contact with one another.

Video with french subtitles & graphics

ソフトウェア開発会社　プロモーション
**Software Development Company
Promotional Brochure**
Belgium　1995

CD : **Sébastien Houtart**

AD, D, I : **Nathalie Pollet**

CW : **Michael Leahy**

DF : **Signé Lazer**

CL : **IBM-Belgium**

SIZE : **170 × 170mm**

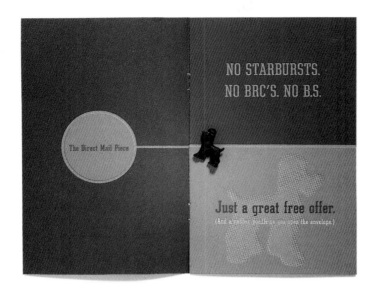

NO STARBURSTS.
NO BRC'S. NO B.S.

The Direct Mail Piece

Just a great free offer.
(And a rubber poodle in you open the envelope.)

YOU CAN GET A 3-USER PACK OF QUICKMAIL™ FOR FREE.

(QuickMail is the #1 Macintosh® e-mail system
and we think you'll really like it.)

Product features: QuickMail lets you quickly send copy back and
forth through your network. QuickMail's QuickConference™ feature lets
you have real-time, on-screen conversations. QuickMail eliminates
the need for paper memos and messages. QuickMail lets you
and receive messages on the road. Product benefit
shields you whenever the office lackey goes on a po
sentences you to death by memo. QuickMail lets you blow
to entire qualm-riddled committees with the simple push of
QuickMail lets you send many ego-muddled diatribes to indiff
AE's. QuickMail lets you keep in touch with esteemed colleag
without actually wasting your time talking to them. QuickMa
improves life, liberty and the pursuit of gold pencils. Reassurances
to ease your jaded, ad-corrupted heart: This offer includes no
catches, strings or other deceptive treacheries. You get the QuickMail
3-user pack for absolutely free and you can use it until you die.
There is no fine print and if you call us, no salesman will visit your
home. Hidden motive: We're just trying to introduce QuickMail
into more advertising agencies because we heard you're all rich.

The Sales Pitch

1.800.523.7638

Call to Action

TAKE ACTION AND CALL TODAY!

1.800.523.7638 (Program CE 301) gets you free QuickMail. And in the
meantime, enjoy your rubbery new pal!
Here's where our big whopping logo
would have gone if our agency had caved.

QuickMail/CE Software, Inc.

P.O. Box 65580, 1801 Industrial Circle, West Des Moines, IA 50265

World Wide Web: http://www.cesoft.com

© 1995 CE Software, Inc. All rights reserved. CE Software, QuickMail and QuickConference are trademarks of CE Software, Inc.

ソフトウェア開発会社　プロモーション
Software Development Company
Promotional Brochure
USA　1995

CD, AD, D, I, CW, DF : **Planet Design Company**

CL : **CE Software Incorporated**

SIZE : **202 × 128mm**

ソフトウェア開発会社　プロモーション
Software Developement Company
Promotional Brochure
Italy　1995

CD, AD, D : **Giona Maiarelli**

CD : **Ann Rathkopf**

P : **Studio Azimut**

CW : **Nico Maccentelli**

DF : **Maiarelli & Rathkopf**

CL : **Integra**

SIZE : **275 × 160mm**

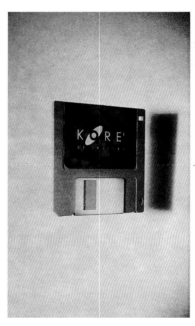

Korè

L'intelligenza

interattiva

nella

produzione

Guarda, elabora e interagisce per darvi sempre un quadro esaustivo delle vostre fasi produttive. Questo è in sintesi Korè. Un Sistema di raccolta dati che non si sostituisce all'organizzazione produttiva pre-esistente, ma che si integra alla perfezione con essa ottimizzandola. Korè è un Sistema interattivo flessibile, perché interviene in tempo reale nelle fasi produttive validando ogni tipo di procedura, rendendola oggettiva, al di là di ogni problematica derivante da fattori umani.

Le soluzioni di Korè.

IL CODICE A BARRE
Caratteristica fondamentale di Korè è il "codice a barre", ossia la raccolta dati mediante rilevatore ottico. Con Korè tale raccolta diviene dunque semplice e veloce, consentendo senza margine di errore di determinare in tempo reale l'ordine di lavorazione, con specifico riferimento non solo alla *fase/risorsa*, ma anche al centro di *costo/lavorazione*.

LE PIATTAFORME
Le piattaforme hardware di Korè, sulle quali si può basare la rilevazione dei dati sono due:
- una per l'impiego di appositi terminali industriali, idonei ad ambienti più severi, dislocati nei punti nevralgici della produzione, con l'utilizzo di lettori ottici, e del codice a barre;
- l'altra è stata ideata per l'inserimento di PC** al posto della terminaleria industriale, consentendo di avere in dotazione uno strumento potente e flessibile e rendendo così la prestazione disponibile per altri utilizzi. Anche questa piattaforma impiega penne ottiche per codici a barre, ma a differenza di molti altri software, è possibile effettuare data-entry manuali, inserendo da tastiera informazioni riguardanti non solo le risorse in produzione, ma anche quelle concernenti uffici tecnici e amministrativi, per un monitoraggio globale della struttura aziendale.
Le soluzioni di Korè dunque, si configurano come un sistema in ogni caso idoneo alle esigenze dei più diversi comparti aziendali. Concepito per sistema operativo Windows™* e sviluppato in ambiente Visual Basic *, con l'utilizzo di DataBase Access *, Korè ha una grafica funzionale e piacevole, che facilita la lettura e la riconoscibilità delle operazioni indicate.

La grafica di Korè, con il sistema operativo Windows™*, consente una lettura immediata del menu generale e una facile comprensione di ogni funzione, realizzando con operazioni semplici e veloci.

Il codice a barre è il sistema più pratico ed efficace per organizzare e uniformare ogni tipo di informazione dal campo. L'associazione tra il codice e l'oggetto/fase/informazione è chiara e viene aggiornato da rilevatori ottici o al centro di costo/lavorazione.

Le funzioni di Korè.
I moduli di Korè consentono una gestione globale dell'organizzazione interna, disponendo di tutte le funzioni base:
- *Gestione archivi base*, dove sono caricati gli ordini di lavorazione e le anagrafiche degli articoli, dei cicli, delle risorse, ecc.
- *Controllo avanzamento produzione*, prevede l'"esplosione" degli ordini di lavorazione e l'individuazione immediata dello stato di avanzamento di ciascuna commessa;
- *Stampe e consuntivi*, consente:
  a) la consuntivazione per ordine di lavoro, risorsa, centro di costo, lavorazione, macchina, ecc.
  b) la quadratura tra presenze e produzione
  c) il controllo dell'avanzamento per ordine di lavoro;
- *Rendimenti*, calcolo dei rendimenti per risorsa, articolo, ordine di lavoro, con relativi scostamenti rispetto agli standard;
- *Grafici*, riporto con modalità grafica dei vari indicatori di rendimento e produzione;
- *Simulatore a capacità infinita*, permette di visualizzare graficamente i "colli di bottiglia" e quindi di pianificare le risorse;
- *Gestione terminali*, consente:
  a) la programmazione locale delle transazioni;
  b) l'impostazione dati con rilevatori ottici (o magnetici);
  c) il prelevamento dei dati con validazione in tempo reale.

ソフトウェア開発会社　製品案内
Software Development Company
Promotional Brochure
USA　1995

AD. D. I : **Kathleen Forsythe**

D : **Shannon Beer**

CW : **Neal Kane**

DF : **Forsythe Design**

CL : **Vivo Software, Inc.**

SIZE : **293 × 215mm**

▼ A Whole New Way to Look at Your PC
(And Talk to It)

The benefits of videoconferencing are easy to understand. The ability to share voice, image, and document information with people in remote locations eliminates many of the time, cost, and logistical issues associated with traditional meetings. However, until now, the investment in space and equipment required to implement a room-based videoconferencing solution has kept this technology beyond the reach of many individuals.

Vivo320™ Personal Videoconferencing truly delivers a view without a room™. With Vivo320, your PC is transformed into a versatile communications center. Vivo Software's groundbreaking H.320 software video technology sets the new price/performance standard in desktop videoconferencing. By doing the video compression/decompression in software, Vivo Software is able to deliver the first affordable, high-performance, H.320 standards-compliant, personal videoconferencing solution.

The Vivo320 solution is a powerful business productivity tool that enables you to conduct face-to-face meetings with anyone, or any group, from the comfort of your own office. By simply installing Vivo's Windows®-based software application and configuring your desktop PC with our convenience kit of off-the-shelf hardware components, Vivo320 virtually eliminates the time and location problems associated with conducting business on a global scale.

▼ A Whole New Way to Look at Your PC
(And Talk to It)

The benefits of videoconferencing are easy to understand. The ability to share voice, image, and document information with people in remote locations eliminates many of the time, cost, and logistical issues associated with traditional meetings. However, until now, the investment in space and equipment required to implement a room-based videoconferencing solution has kept this technology beyond the reach of many individuals.

Vivo320™ Personal Videoconferencing truly delivers a view without a room™. With Vivo320, your PC is transformed into a versatile communications center. Vivo Software's groundbreaking H.320 software video technology sets the new price/performance standard in desktop videoconferencing. By doing the video compression/decompression in software, Vivo Software is able to deliver the first affordable, high-performance, H.320 standards-compliant, personal videoconferencing solution.

The Vivo320 solution is a powerful business productivity tool that enables you to conduct face-to-face meetings with anyone, or any group, from the comfort of your own office. By simply installing Vivo's Windows®-based software application and configuring your desktop PC with our convenience kit of off-the-shelf hardware components, Vivo320 virtually eliminates the time and location problems associated with conducting business on a global scale.

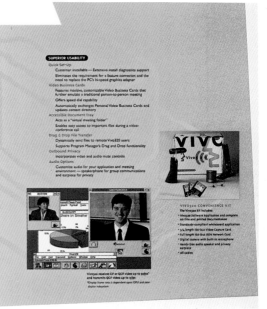

▼ Why Choose Vivo320?

STATE OF THE ART TECHNOLOGY

Industry's First Software Compression/Decompression (Codec)
- Offers superior video compression implementation
- Allows other applications to run simultaneously
- Removes dependence on costly hardware codec components
- Automatically performs better on more powerful processors
- Enables easy access to performance improvements through software upgrades
- Long term investment which grows in value over time

UNIVERSAL INTEROPERABILITY

H.320 Standards-Compliant
- Complies with the universally-adopted ITU-T interoperability standard for videoconferencing
- Enables participation in remote group meetings with all H.320-compliant group and personal videoconferencing systems installed worldwide
Dynamic Rate Adaptation
- Automatically adapts to 112 or 128 Kbps transmission rates
- Ensures that national and international calls get through
ScreenView
- Delivers high-quality audio/visual presentations directly from your PC to remote PCs and group videoconferencing systems
- Eliminates the need for document cameras and the necessity to fax PC-generated information prior to video calls
- Works during point-to-point and multi-point calls
Multi-Point Videoconferencing
- Enables participation in H.320 multi-point conference calls
- Interoperates with all H.320 multi-point services

OPEN SYSTEM DESIGN

Virtual Communications Port
- Easily integrates with other vendors' whiteboard and application sharing products, as well as any Windows-based product that runs over a communications port
- Allows quick access to your chosen collaborative application during videoconferencing calls
Versatile Hardware Components
- Utilizes off-the-shelf, multi-purpose PC boards
- Leverages multi-purpose boards for applications other than videoconferencing

SUPERIOR USABILITY

Quick Set-Up
- Customer installable — Extensive install diagnostics support
- Eliminates the requirement for a feature connector, and the need to replace the PC's hi-speed graphics adaptor
Video Business Cards
- Features intuitive, customizable Video Business Cards that further emulate a traditional person-to-person meeting
- Offers speed dial capability
- Automatically exchanges Personal Video Business Cards and updates contact directory
Accessible Document Tray
- Acts as a "virtual meeting folder"
- Enables easy access to important files during a videoconference call
Drag & Drop File Transfer
- Dynamically send files to remote Vivo320 users
- Supports Program Manager's Drag and Drop functionality
Outbound Privacy
- Incorporates video and audio mute controls
Audio Options
- Customize audio for your application and meeting environment — speakerphone for group communications and earpiece for privacy

VIVO320 CONVENIENCE KIT
The Vivo320 kit includes:
- Vivo320 software application and complete on-line and printed documentation
- Standards-compliant whiteboard application
- 3/4 length ISA-bus Video Capture Card
- Full length ISA-bus ISDN Network Card
- Digital camera with built-in microphone
- Hands-free audio speaker and privacy earpiece
- All cables

Vivo320 receives CIF or QCIF video up to 30fps* and transmits QCIF video up to 15fps.
*Display frame rate is dependent upon CPU and your display subsystem.

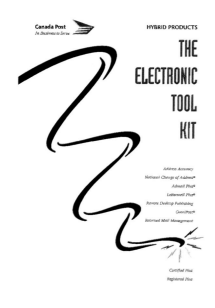

郵便局　新サービス案内
Post Office　New Services Information
Canada　1994

CD : **John Staresinic**

AD : **Don Raabe**

D : **Tim Cearns**

I : **John Day**

DF : **Acart**

CL : **Canada Post Corporation**

SIZE : **317 × 207mm**

Communicate.
Collaborate.
Coordinate.

**The POWER to
Communicate key information.**

Lotus Notes® gives you the power you need to communicate within and beyond your organization. If you need to communicate with suppliers, customers and partners at other companies using different e-mail systems, or reach them via the Internet®, it is easy with Lotus Notes. Mobile Notes users can "take their desktop" along with them – transforming airports, hotels and cars into workspaces complete with up-to-the-minute information. And now, the Lotus Notes product family includes the world's most reliable and innovative client/server messaging system; Notes Mail®, which incorporates the world's most popular messaging user interface, ccMail®.

**The POWER to
Collaborate on projects
and share information.**

Lotus Notes goes beyond traditional e-mail. With Notes™ you can collaborate and share ideas with team members on joint projects, access bulletin boards, participate in group discussions, create document libraries, access news databases and send and receive e-mail. Rather than waiting for an e-mail message to come to you, with Notes you have the power to find the information you need just when you need it.

**The POWER to
Coordinate critical business processes.**

Lotus Notes is the next logical step from electronic mail to a single cost-effective infrastructure for electronic messaging and groupware. Lotus Notes lets you create custom business applications that coordinate everyday business processes from start to finish to achieve results – like improving customer service, making your sales force more productive, getting products to market faster, and managing your most valuable asset, your people. Lotus Notes customers consistently find significant payback on their Notes investment. According to an independent study, Notes users have achieved an average of 179% annual return on their investment.*

"If I could only choose one software application,
I would choose Lotus Notes."

Fireman's Fund Insurance — Virgil Pittman

* * International Data Corporation, "Lotus Notes – Agent of Change, The Financial Impact of Lotus Notes on Business."

Solutions

**Lotus Notes breaks down the
barriers to effective teamwork.**

Lotus Notes is the world's leading messaging and groupware product. Millions of people in thousands of companies are using Notes today to break down traditional barriers and create alliances that extend across departments and beyond the walls of the organization. Its teams of employees, customers, suppliers and business partners have simultaneous access to the information they need, no matter where they're located or what computer platform they are using.

**Turn customer service
into a strategic advantage.**

Lotus Notes connects you more tightly with your customers to foster customer loyalty. Your service representatives can tap into a Notes database for up-to-date information to answer a customer question or provide an instant response. Everyone who comes in contact with the customer can review each customer's history and view all the information associated with that customer to get a complete picture. With Notes you can incorporate information from relational databases or legacy systems such as accounts receivable and order processing. The information can be easily updated, and labor-intensive tasks like correspondence can be automated. Customer service information is available to other departments and can even be made available directly to customers if you choose. With Notes you can service more customers faster, turning superior customer service into a competitive advantage.

**Notes opens doors
and closes sales.**

Notes energizes your sales team. It provides everything from the hottest leads and latest competitive information to new product specifications and up-to-the-minute pricing. Automating your sales flow with Notes gives them the ability to take more of their office with them on the road. They can continue working while disconnected from the network, and dial in anytime to automatically receive and send the latest information. With Notes you can make better decisions and immediately respond to opportunities. You can centralize information about the competition to help spot trends and respond to competitive challenges. Speed response to customer inquiries. Submit orders, discuss pricing, and route purchase orders from any location. Notes helps streamline every aspect of the sales process.

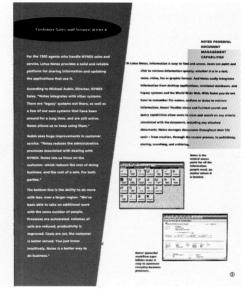

Customer Sales and Service: NYNEX

For the 1500 agents who handle NYNEX sales and service, Lotus Notes provides a solid and reliable platform for sharing information and updating the applications that use it.

According to Michael Aubin, Director, NYNEX Sales. "Notes integrates with other systems. There are 'legacy' systems out there, as well as a few of our own systems that have been around for a long time, and are still active. Notes allows us to keep using them."

Aubin sees huge improvements in customer service. "Notes reduces the administrative processes associated with dealing with NYNEX. Notes lets us focus on the customer, which reduces the cost of doing business, and the cost of a sale. For both parties."

The bottom line is the ability to do more with less, over a larger region. "We've been able to take on additional work with the same number of people. Processes are automated, volumes of calls are reduced, productivity is improved. Costs are cut, the customer is better served. You just know intuitively, Notes is a better way to do business."

**NOTES POWERFUL
DOCUMENT
MANAGEMENT
CAPABILITIES**

With Lotus Notes, information is easy to find and access. Users can point and click to retrieve information quickly, whether it is in a text, voice, video, fax or graphic format. And Notes easily integrates information from desktop applications, relational databases, and legacy systems and the World Wide Web. With Notes you do not have to remember file names, authors or dates to retrieve information. Notes' flexible views and full-text search and query capabilities allow users to view and search on any criteria associated with the document, including any attached documents. Notes manages documents throughout their life cycle – from creation, through the review process, to publishing, storing, searching, and archiving.

THE POWER of people
WORKING together

Now is
the time
for
Lotus
Notes

**It Is Easy
To Get Started With
Notes**

**Notes gives you
your choice of functionality.**

Lotus Notes provides you with three licensing options for building a unified groupware infrastructure: Lotus Notes Mail, Lotus Notes Desktop, and Lotus Notes.

Lotus Notes Mail.

Notes Mail is a state-of-the-art, client/server messaging system. Notes Mail includes the ccMail user interface, OLE 2.0 support, platform independent viewers, collapsible sections, the InterNotes Web Navigator, task management, document libraries, personal journal, phone messages, and unparalleled mobile user support.

Lotus Notes Desktop.

Lotus Notes Desktop is a run-time Notes client with the ability to run any Notes application. Notes Desktop enables you to extend your most strategic applications to everyone in your workgroup. Includes Notes Mail functionality and simple application templates. Notes Desktop is an affordable solution ideal for Notes users who need to access customized applications.

Lotus Notes:

Lotus Notes gives you the full-function power to create custom applications for improving the quality of everyday business processes. Includes an application development environment, system administration capabilities and Notes Mail functionality.

**Build your Notes system
as you build your business.**

Start with the core capabilities of Lotus Notes and build strategic business process applications for your workgroup. Tailor your application development, database and messaging capabilities as your needs change and your workgroup expands.

There's a rapidly-growing industry of value-added software products and services based on Lotus Notes. Choose from hundreds of off-the-shelf applications or work with one of the 11,000 Lotus Business Partners to customize an application appropriate for your company.

**GROUP SCHEDULING IS
EASY WITH LOTUS
ORGANIZER AND NOTES**

Lotus Organizer® uses existing Notes and ccMail directories to set up group meetings and address meeting notices. There is no faster or easier way to manage your workload, stay in touch with business contacts, and schedule meetings, than with Lotus Organizer and Notes.

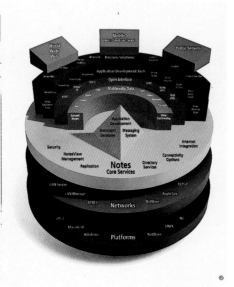

ソフトウェア開発会社　製品案内
**Software Development Company
Promotional Brochure**
USA　1995

AD : **Kathleen Forsythe**

D : **Shannon Beer**

P : **Logan Seale**

DF : **Forsythe Design**

CL : **Lotus Corporation**

SIZE : **280 × 215mm**

フォントメーカー 製品案内　Font Designer　Promotional Materials　USA　1996
CD, AD, D：**Carlos Segura**　DF：**Segura Inc.**　CL：**[t-26]**　SIZE：**300×196mm**

製紙メーカー　プロモーション
Paper Manufacturer　Promotional Brochure
USA　1993

CD, D : **Joel Katz**

D : **David Schpok**

P : **Jenny Lynn / Edward Matalon /
Scott Morgan / Michael Northedge**

I : **Jeff Brice / Steven Guarnaccia /
John Hersey / Lance Hidy / Steven Lyons**

DF : **Paradigm:design**

CL : **Monadnock Paper Mills, Inc.**

SIZE : **305 × 206mm**

フォントメーカー　製品案内
Font Maker　Promotional Brochure
USA　1995

CD, AD, D：**Carlos Segura**

D：**Brenda Rotheiser**

DF：**Segura Inc.**

CL：**AGFA**

SIZE：**264 × 176mm**

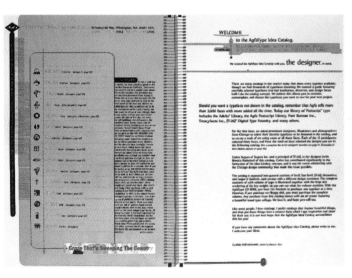

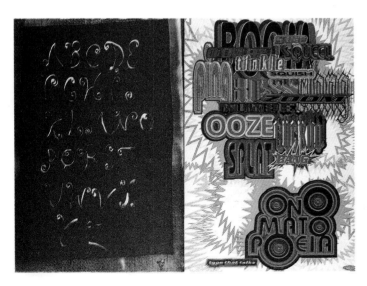

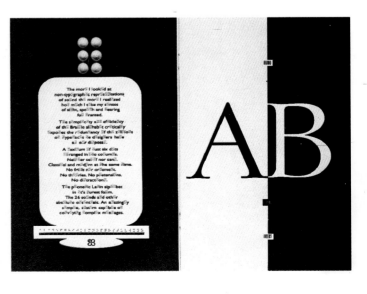

紙会社　プロモーション
Paper Company　Promotional Brochure
USA　1995

CD, AD, D, I : **John Sayles**

P : **Bill Nellans**

CW : **Wendy Lyons**

DF : **Sayles Graphic Design**

CL : **James River Corporation**

SIZE : **305 × 229mm**

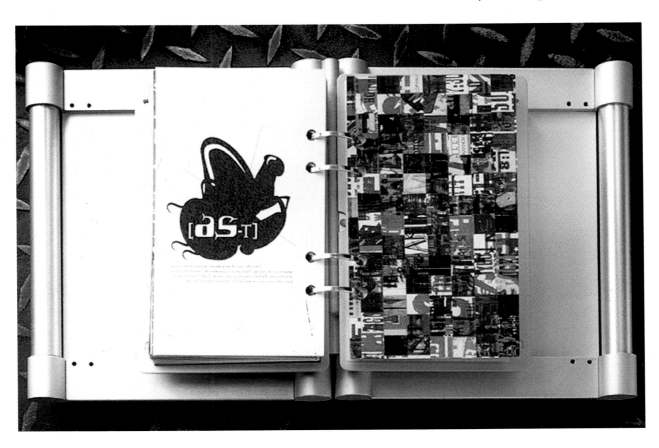

フォントメーカー　製品案内　Font Designer　Product Brochure　USA　1995
CD, AD, D : **Carlos Segura**　DF : **Segura Inc.**　CL : **[t-26]**　SIZE : **270×180mm**

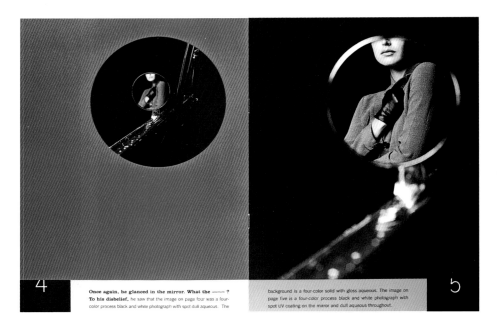

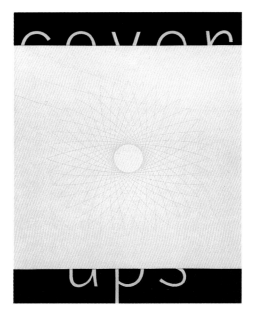

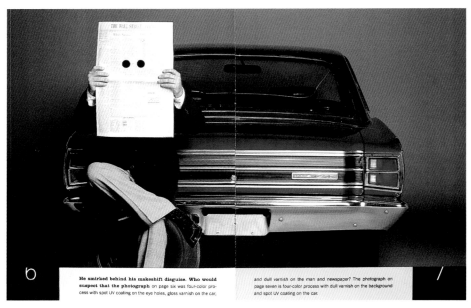

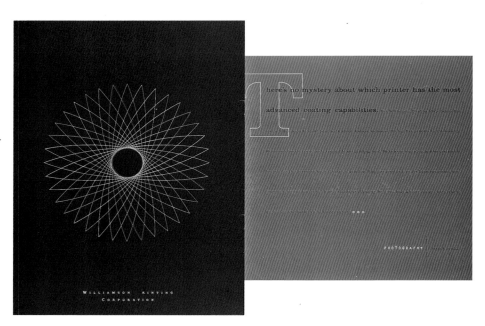

印刷会社　コーティングプロモーション
Printing Company　Promotional Brochure
USA　1995

CD : **Ron Sullivan**

AD, D : **Rob Wilson**

P : **Fredrik Brodén**

CW : **Michael Langley / Mark Perkins**

DF : **Sullivan Perkins**

CL : **Williamson Printing Co.**

SIZE : **300 × 228mm**

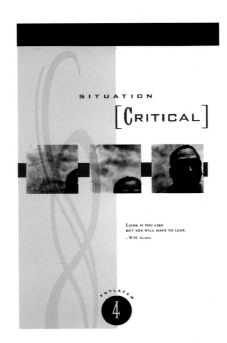

製紙メーカー　プロモーション
Paper Manufacturer　Promotional Brochure
USA　1993

CD, AD, D : **Petrula Vrontikis**

P : **Tim Jones / Everard Williams Jr. /
Paul Ottengheime / Abrams / Lacanina**

CW : **Victoria Branch**

DF : **Vrontikis Design Office**

CL : **Potlatch Corporation**

SIZE : **279×177mm**

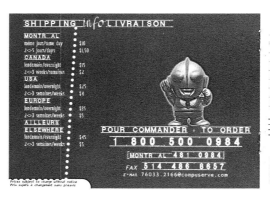

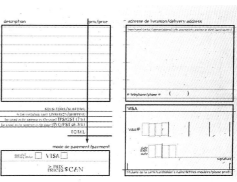

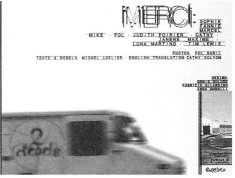

フォント会社　商品案内
Digital Type Foundry　Font Catalogue
Canada　1995

AD, D : **Denis Dulude / Fabrizio Gilardino /**
　　　Anna Morelli

P : **Pol Baril**

CW : **Michel Loslier**

CL : **2 Rebels · Montreal（Québec）**

SIZE : **130 × 180mm**

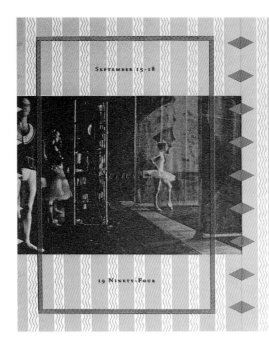

1

1. バレエ団　公演案内
Ballet Company　Season Brochure
USA　1994

CD, AD, D, I, DF : **Planet Design Company**

P : **Image Studios**

CW : **John Anderson**

CL : **Milwaukee Ballet**

SIZE : **305 × 214mm**

2. バレエ団　公演案内
Ballet Company　Season Brochure
USA　1993

CD, AD, D, I, DF : **Planet Design Company**

P : **Richard Brodzeller**

CW : **John Anderson**

CL : **Milwaukee Ballet**

SIZE : **203 × 203mm**

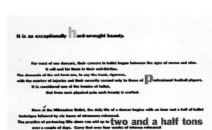

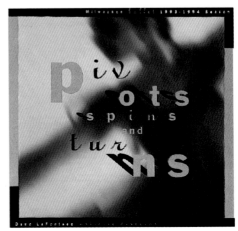

2

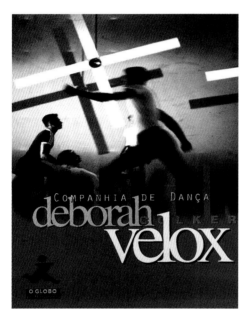

新聞社　ダンス団プロモーション
Newspaper Publisher
Dance Company Promotion
Brasil　1995

CD, AD, D : **Gustavo Portela**

P : **Flavio Cocker / Cafi**

DF : **Interface Designers**

CL : **O Globo Newspaper**

SIZE : **280 × 210mm**

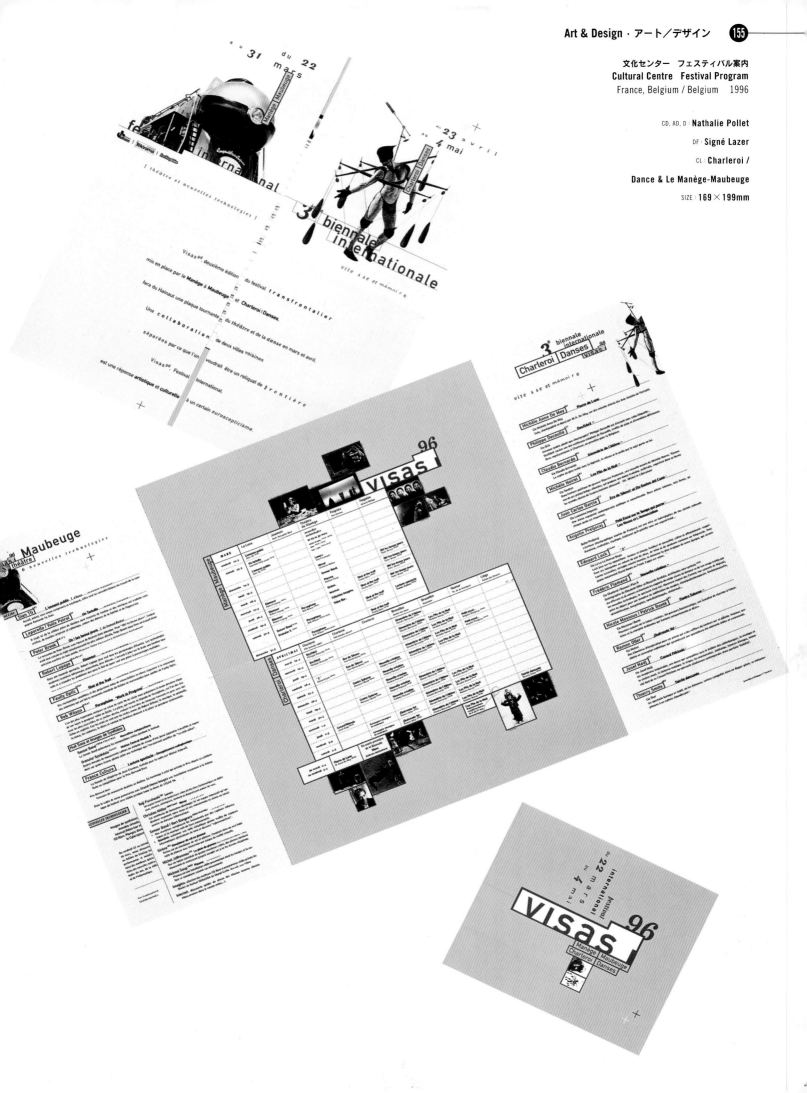

文化センター　フェスティバル案内
Cultural Centre　Festival Program
France, Belgium / Belgium　1996

CD, AD, D : **Nathalie Pollet**

DF : **Signé Lazer**

CL : **Charleroi /**

Dance & Le Manège-Maubeuge

SIZE : **169 × 199mm**

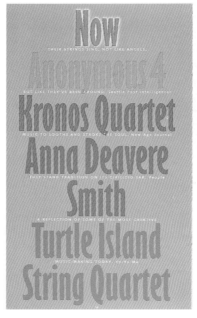

アートセンター　スケジュール
Arts Center　Schedule
USA　1994

CD, AD, D : **John Ball**

I : **John Jinks**

DF : **Mires Design, Inc.**

CL : **California Center for the Arts, Escondido**

SIZE : **323 × 189mm**

アートセンター　スケジュール
Arts Center　Schedule
USA　1995

CD, AD, D : John Ball

I : Gerald Bustamante

DF : Mires Design, Inc.

CL : California Center for the Arts, Escondido

SIZE : 298 × 191mmn

劇場 スケジュール
Theatre Schedule
USA 1995

CD, CW : **Roxy Moffitt**

AD, D : **Robynne Raye / Michael Strassburger**

P : **Kathleen King / Chris Bennion /
Debra. La Coppola**

I : **Brad Holland / Glenn Mitsui /
Andi Rusu / Vittorio Costarella**

CW : **Mark Bocek / Shane Evans**

DF : **Modern Dog**

CL : **Seattle Repertory Theatre**

SIZE : **155×180mm**

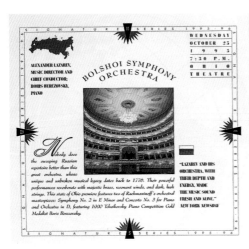

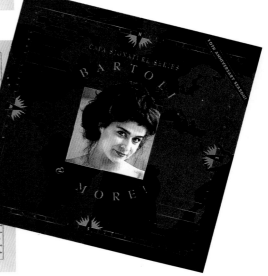

劇場　イベントスケジュール
**Performing Arts Association
Events Schedule**
USA　1995

CD, AD, D : **Eric Rickabaugh**

CW : **Rosia Stolz**

DF : **Rickabaugh Graphics**

CL : **Columbus Association
for the Performing Arts**

SIZE : **215 × 215mm**

アート／デザイン協会　セミナー案内
Art / Design Association　Seminar Invitation
USA　1993

CD, AD, D, I, DF : **Planet Design Company**

CL : **Design Milwaukee**

SIZE : **342 × 241mm**

The 1993 **How Design Conference** on Business and The Creative Process.
April 25th thru 28th, 1993. The Westin Hotel, Chicago, Illinois.

デザイン協議会　情報誌
**Design Conference
Informative Magazine**
USA　1993

CD, AD, D : **Carlos Segura**

DF : **Segura Inc.**

CL : **How**

SIZE : **210×153mm**

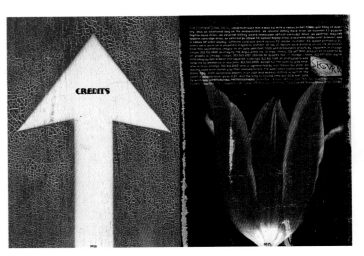

Made in the Midwest: Walter Hamady's 6451 Students. The Development of a Midwest Center for the Book Arts. A monograph published in conjunction with an exhibition at Charles A. Wustum Museum of Fine Arts Racine, Wisconsin.

March 21–May 2, 1993

PARTICIPATE BY SENDING WORK AND A STATEMENT ABOUT THEIR STUDIO AND CLASSROOM EXPERIENCES WITH WALTER HAMADY. THOSE STATEMENTS ARE PART OF THE BIOGRAPHICAL PAGES OF THIS MONOGRAPH. WE THANK THESE EXHIBITORS FOR THEIR ACTIVE PARTICIPATION IN THIS EXHIBITION AND WALTER HAMADY FOR HIS SUPPORT OF THIS PROJECT.

I PARTICULARLY WISH TO THANK THE PEOPLE WHO MADE CONTRIBUTIONS TO SUPPORT THE CREATION OF THIS MONOGRAPH: KAREN JOHNSON BOYD; WALTER HAMADY; DANA LYTLE AND KEVIN WADE OF PLANET DESIGN, MADISON; FRANK PALUCH AND PERIMETER GALLERY, CHICAGO; NORMA RUBOVITS; JOHN WILDE; LESLIE PAPER AND LITHO PRODUCTIONS, MADISON. WE ARE ALSO GRATEFUL TO PROFESSOR WILLIAM BUNCE OF THE KOHLER ART LIBRARY, UNIVERSITY OF WISCONSIN-MADISON, FOR HIS COOPERATION AND SPECIAL SUPPORT. I WISH TO ACKNOWLEDGE AND THANK THE WUSTUM STAFF FOR THEIR ASSISTANCE IN MAKING THIS EXHIBITION POSSIBLE AND IN PARTICULAR, MY ASSOCIATE CURATOR, CAREN HEFT FOR HER DEDICATION TO THIS EFFORT AND HER TIRELESS WORK ON BEHALF OF THE SHOW AND THE PRODUCTION OF THIS MONOGRAPH. WITH THIS EXHIBITION WUSTUM MUSEUM HONORS WALTER HAMADY AND HIS FORMER STUDENTS. THE MUSEUM PLANS TO CONTINUE ITS SUPPORT OF BOOK ARTS AND THE ARTISTS COMMITTED TO THIS METHOD OF WORKING. WE BELIEVE IT IS TRULY A DEMOCRATIC ART FORM WHICH HAS RICH VISUAL AND LITERARY BENEFITS TO OFFER TO AN AUDIENCE WHICH WE HOPE TO ASSIST IN DEVELOPING IN THE COMING YEARS THROUGH MORE EXHIBITIONS AND PUBLICATIONS SUCH AS THIS.

Bruce W. Pepich, Director

Charles A. Wustum Museum of Fine Arts

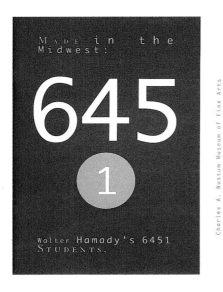

MADE in the Midwest:

645
1

Walter Hamady's 6451 STUDENTS.

Charles A. Wustum Museum of Fine Arts

TYPOGRAPHERS HELP THE LESS EXPERIENCED, AND CARRIES OVER INTO POST-STUDENT LIFE. IN THIS EXHIBITION THE VIEWER WILL SEE THAT MOST OF THE BOOKS PRESENTED ARE COLLABORATIVE IN ONE FORM OR ANOTHER. A SINGLE BOOK CAN BOAST OF A TYPOGRAPHER, A WRITER, ILLUSTRATOR, BINDER, EVEN CALLIGRAPHER, WORKING TOGETHER TO CREATE THIS WORK. MANY FORMER STUDENTS CONTINUE COLLABORATIVE EFFORTS BEGUN AT MADISON: WALTER TISDALE, PATI SCOBEY AND KATHY KUEHN CONTINUE TO MAKE WORK TOGETHER, AS DO OTHERS.

COMPULSIVE CRAFTSMANSHIP is another common thread in Hamady's former students. HE IS THE CONSUMMATE MEASURE AGAINST WHOM THEY MUST STRETCH THEMSELVES. "...HE WILL ALWAYS BE THE PRINTER AGAINST WHOM I MEASURE MY ACCOMPLISHMENTS." THE CARE THAT GOES INTO A BOOK CAN BE SEEN BY EXAMINING THE PROOF COPY AND FINISHED COPY OF MARGARET SUNDAY'S BOOK *Words of the Teacher*. BARBARA TETENBAUM'S *Stick Book*, IN WHICH SHE COMBINES PAPERMAKING, STRUCTURE AND CONTENT, AND SHIEBE MELIN'S *Comparative Anatomy of the Heart*, ALSO EXHIBIT THAT HIGH LEVEL OF CRAFTSMANSHIP FOR WHICH HAMADY IS FAMOUS.

WORDS FORM AN IMPORTANT PART OF MOST OF THE BOOKS IN THIS EXHIBITION. ONE OF HAMADY'S REQUIREMENTS IS THAT HIS STUDENTS MAKE BOOKS AND BROADSIDES THAT FEATURE ORIGINAL, UNPUBLISHED WRITING, WHICH CATAPULTS THE STUDENT INTO LITERATURE IN THE SEARCH FOR MATERIAL. THE RESULTS OF THIS ARE FAR-REACHING. FLEDGLING BOOKMAKERS BECOME AWARE OF THE VALUE OF WORDS, BECOME JUDGMENTAL IN THEIR APPROACH TO WRITING, AND BECOME INVOLVED IN THE VAST LITERARY WORLD OF THE LATE TWENTIETH CENTURY. HAMADY HIMSELF HAS COLLABORATED WITH SUCH WRITERS AS TOBY OLSON, WHILE HIS FORMER STUDENTS WORK WITH EQUALLY WELL-KNOWNS, SUCH AS PABLO NERUDA AND JEROME ROTHENBERG.

WORDS ARE IMPORTANT TO CHARLES ALEXANDER, AN ENGLISH MAJOR WHO SOMEHOW FOUND HIS WAY INTO HAMADY'S CLASS AND WAS SUBVERTED INTO BOOKMAKING. HE IS THE FOUNDER AND EXECUTIVE DIRECTOR OF THE CHAX PRESS, A NON-PROFIT ORGANIZATION WHICH PUBLISHES INNOVATIVE CONTEMPORARY WRITING IN BOOK ARTS AND LITERARY TRADE EDITION. HIS TRAINING AS A BOOKMAKER HAS THUS BEEN BROUGHT TO THE WORLD OF PUBLISHING AND LITERATURE.

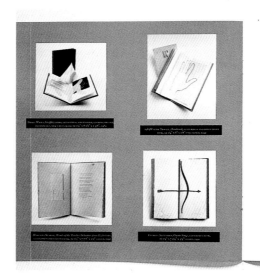

美術館　展覧会カタログ
Museum　Exhibition Monograph
USA　1993

CD, AD, D, I, DF : **Planet Design Company**

CL : **Charles A. Wustum Museum**

SIZE : **254 × 217mm**

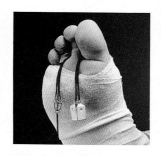

R I A N D E J O N G
AMULET
zilver / messing
‹Talloze dingen gebeuren ook zonder woorden›

R I C H A R D W A L R A V E N
AMANDELEN ONGEPELD
‹158 gram amandelen, getransformeerd tot halssieraad door ze met binddraad aan
elkaar te rijgen. Als sluiting een gouden oog›

M E C K Y V A N D E N B R I N K
MET GROENE STIP
silicium / schudketting

P E G G Y B A N N E N B E R G
MAZZEL-MOSSEL
*mossels / parels / verguld koper / zijdedraad / zilver /
bladgoud / t-shirt / textielverf*

J E A N L E M M E N S
Japanse lak op hout / eierschaalinleg / zilver
‹Een dans op een heuveltje. / Boodschapper tussen hemel en aarde.
Naar de vier windstreken. / De naam van de nieuwe koning.
Rijdier van de Sjamaan. / Toverstokje · Wandelstokje›

R U U D T P E T E R S
TOELA
zilver / steenkool

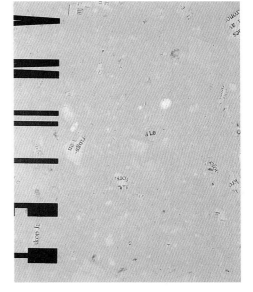

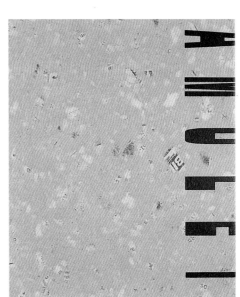

ギャラリー　コレクションカタログ
Gallery　Promotional Brochure
The Netherlands　1993

CD, D : **Henrik Barends**

P : **Tono Stano**

DF : **Studio Henrik Barends**

CL : **Galerie Marzee**

SIZE : **135 × 105mm**

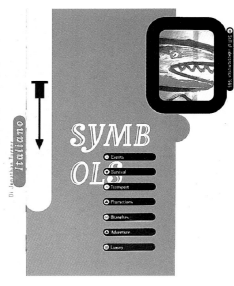

Andy Warhol ha detto: "La business art è l'immediato conseguenza dell'arte." Negli Anni Novanta, Int. Fish-handel SERVAAS & Zn. si concentra sull'arte della gestione strategica. La compagnia nacque fra due mondi finanziari separati. Ha stretti rapporti non solo con il Ministero della Cultura ma anche con la Camera di Commercio. Come prevedibile, Servaas riceve sovvenzioni da musei d'arte di tutto il mondo. Come piccolo imprenditore di mandati artistici ottiene speciali esenzioni fiscali. Ma in un momento in cui i valori tradizionali vengono regolarmente sostituiti dagli interessi commerciali, tutto ciò non è poi una gran sorpresa. L'ambiguità d'arrivi una regola.

"Che differenza c'è tra Miami Vice e il Telegiornale? Cos'è più reale? Quando i miei lavori appaiono in t.v., la gente crede che siano veri." Ho molto tempo fa, Servaas è apparso in un documentario tedesco. Nel filmato, pescava da una barca in un canale olandese, con un mulino a vento sullo sfondo. Il pesce marino che pinza è chiaramente morto, acquistato nella pescheria locale e attaccato all'amo. Così, anche i più affidabili biografi cadono nella trappola dei comportamenti fraudolenti.

"E così è l'arte dopo tutto? Un tramonto norvegese è arte. Lo spot pubblicitario che ti dice che Gino Lava mille volte più bianco, è arte. I musei e le gallerie hanno di interessarsi soltanto di arte, ma quando si svolta di soldi, è tutta un'altra faccenda. E se arte è uguale a denaro, allora non c'è nessuna differenza tra avere una pescheria e dipingere un quadro."

"Io non parlo solo di arte. Fra scuole anni l'idea stessa dell'arte sarebbe non esistere più. In ogni caso, non sarà intesa nello stesso modo. L'arte sarà un hobby come un altro."

Nel frattempo, Int. fish-handel SERVAAS & Zn. continua ad inaugurare nuovi filiali: a Porto, Monaco, Basilea e Milano. La sua immagine aziendale si consolida, ma è dubbio oriare. Infatti, è facile sapere non si è acquistato, ma non come classificarle.

Di Jonathan Turner — *italiani*

SYMB OLS
- Events
- Survival
- Transport
- Promotions
- Branches
- Adventure
- Luxury

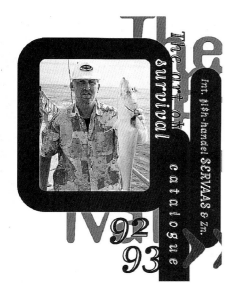

The art on survival catalogue — *Int. Fish-handel SERVAAS & Zn.*

92 93

Dial now! Order now!

Dial now! Order now!

ギャラリー　展示品カタログ
Art Gallery　Promotional Brochure
The Netherlands / Singapore　1993

D : **Paul van der Veer / Nathalie Arts**

P : **S. Steal / H. de Weerd / R. Beemsterboer**

CW : **Jonathan Turner**

CL : **de la Tour / Galerie**

SIZE : **254 × 210mm**

アートセンター　イベントスケジュール
Art Center　Event Schedule
USA　1990

CD, AD, D, I, DF : **Planet Design Company**

CL : **Madison Art Center**

SIZE : **192 × 283mm**

LEOPOLDO PLENTZ

J.R. DURAN

SEBASTIÃO SALGADO

LUIZ HUMBERTO

PEDRO MARTINELLI

KATIA MINDLIN LEITE SAMPAIO / SOTHEBY'S

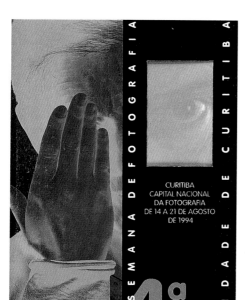

4ª SEMANA DE FOTOGRAFIA · CIDADE DE CURITIBA

CURITIBA
CAPITAL NACIONAL
DA FOTOGRAFIA
DE 14 A 21 DE AGOSTO
DE 1994

4ª

brincando COM A LUZ

MIGUEL CHIKAOKA

W13 PROGRAMA

batalha CONTRA A mediocridade

MARTIN PARR

W14

anos luz

LUIZ BRAGA

Nadja Peregrino

os trabalhadores

SEBASTIÃO SALGADO

地方自治体　展覧会カタログ
Mayor's Office　Art Exhibition Brochure
Brasil　1994

CD, AD, D, I : **Silvio Silva Junior**

P : **Urban**

CW, DF : **Studio Lúmen**

CL : **Fundação Cultural de Curitiba**

SIZE : **280 × 200mm**

アートセンター　展覧会カタログ
Arts Center　Exhibition Brochure
USA　1995

CD, AD, D：**John Ball**

D：**Gale Spitzley**

CW：**Reesey Shaw**

DF：**Mires Design, Inc.**

CL：**California Center for the Arts Museum**

SIZE：**279×279mm**

The **Rock and Roll Hall of Fame** was launched in 1983, when the music industry decided the time had come to honor the men and women who had made significant contributions to the history of rock and roll. Spearheaded by Atlantic Records founder Ahmet Ertegun and a small group of musically obsessed industry leaders (including Rolling Stone Editor and Publisher Jann S. Wenner, Sire Records President Seymour Stein, Elektra Entertainment Chairman Bob Krasnow, attorney Allen Grubman, Atlantic Records Vice-President Noreen Woods, and attorney Suzan Evans, who became executive director of the Foundation), the Rock and Roll Hall of Fame Foundation was created both to honor the artists (and the non-performers) who have shaped rock and roll and to document the historical importance of the music itself. After establishing the rules of eligibility and the procedures for election, the Hall of Fame Foundation held its first induction ceremony at the Waldorf Astoria Hotel in New York in 1986. The first class of inductees was composed of the cream of rock's founding fathers: Chuck Berry, James Brown, Ray Charles, Sam Cooke, Fats Domino, the Everly Brothers, Buddy Holly, Jerry Lee Lewis, Elvis Presley and Little Richard. In addition, legendary DJ Alan Freed and Sun Records founder Sam Phillips were inducted as non-performers; Robert Johnson, Jimmie Rodgers and Jimmy Yancey were honored under the early influences category. Producer and talent scout John Hammond was given a special lifetime achievement award. Since then, membership in the Hall of Fame has expanded to include more than 100 rock legends, and the annual induction ceremony has become one of the key events on the music industry calendar. Like rock and roll itself, the event crosses generational and cultural boundaries to make pioneers of today's innovative artists. Bob Dylan, Little Richard, Chuck Berry, Keith Richards, Mick Jagger, Bruce Springsteen, John Fogerty, Robbie Robertson, Pete Townshend, Bono and Sting are just a few of the many artists who have made the induction ceremony such a momentous occasion and a true reflection of the Hall of Fame's international significance.

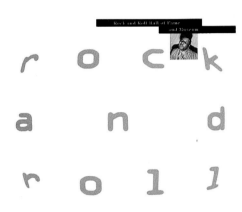

美術館　プロモーション
Museum   Promotional Brochure
USA　1994

CD, AD, D : **Mark Schwartz / Joyce Nesnadny**

D : **Brian Lavy / Michelle Moehler**

P : **Tony Festa Photography**

CW : **Resnicow Schroeder Associates**

DF : **Nesnadny + Schwartz**

CL : **Rock and Roll Hall of Fame / Museum**

SIZE : **286 × 246mm**

Metalli moderni

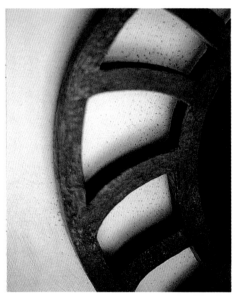

Morigi Restauri

Materiali archeologici

美術品修復会社　プロモーション
Restoration Firm　Promotional Brochure
Italy　1994

CD, AD, D : **Giona Maiarelli**

CD, AD : **Ann Rathkopf**

P : **Giovanni Morigi**

DF : **Maiarelli & Rathkopf**

CL : **Giovanni Morigi & Figlio**

SIZE : **300 × 230mm**

This exhibition was
organized by the
California Center for
the Arts Museum.

Published by the California
Center for the Arts Museum
340 North Escondido Boulevard
Escondido, CA 92025

Library of Congress
Catalog Card Number: 95-08856

ISBN 1-885086-02-7

Printed in the
United States

California Center for
the Arts Museum
May 21 through August 25, 1995

Peter Shelton

Robert Therrien

Mary Bates

Rob Craigie

Tom Driscoll

California:
In Three
Dimensions

Mineko Grimmer

Tim Hawkinson

Jay Johnson

Tina Hulett

Lere

Anne Mudge

Tomas Nakada

Minoru Ohira

Melissa Smedley

Peter Walker

University: Alfred, New York, 1986–90

Photography
Heart of Darkness by Joseph Conrad
The history of clay
Garden
Containers
Val, Roger, Elisa and Alison
Childhood
My Dinner with Andre
The History of Sculpture
The work of H.C. Westermann

Mills College: Oakland, California, 1990–92
John Baldessari: SFMOMA, July 12–September 9, 1990
Idea
Boxes
Honeybees and hives
Beeswax
Natural color
Smell
Breath
Individual personality
Air
Air pumps
The work of Joseph Beuys
Energy
Containment
Bottles

Haines Gallery San Francisco: 1992–Present
Laboratory/Studio
Alone
Looking at the air in a basketball
Eyeballs and various body parts
Words for objects
Inventories for projects
Vocabulary
Work as one
The World as I See It by Albert Einstein
Eye color
Clot
Kool-Aid
Thinking is Form: The Drawings of Joseph Beuys:
MOCA, Los Angeles, CA 1993
Female beauty
Sublime Air Clot: Haines Gallery SF, September 7–October 2, 1993
Black eyes
Laboratory pets
Short Cuts: Stories by Raymond Carver, Movie by Robert Altman
Frankenstein by Mary Shelley
Salubrious Air Clot Experiment:
Toronto, Canada, November 17–December 31, 1994
Demiurgic
Autonomy
Leaking heart
The history of philosophy
Simplicity
Non-art public
Experiment:
732 Market St.: Haines Gallery SF, January 12–February 18, 1995

Rob Craigie

Page 170
アートセンター　展覧会カタログ
Arts Center　Exhibition Brochure
USA　1995

CD, AD, D : **John Ball**

D : **Deborah Hom**

DF : **Mires Design, Inc.**

CL : **California Center for the Arts Museum**

SIZE : **305 × 202mm**

デザインコレクション会社　プロモーション
Design Collective Company　Design Promotion
Belgium　1995

CD, AD, D : **Jo Klaps / Simon Jones**

CD, AD, D, CW : **Ick Reuvis**

P : **Eddy Fliers**

DF : **Gdd**

CL : **Labo**

SIZE : **230 × 130mm**

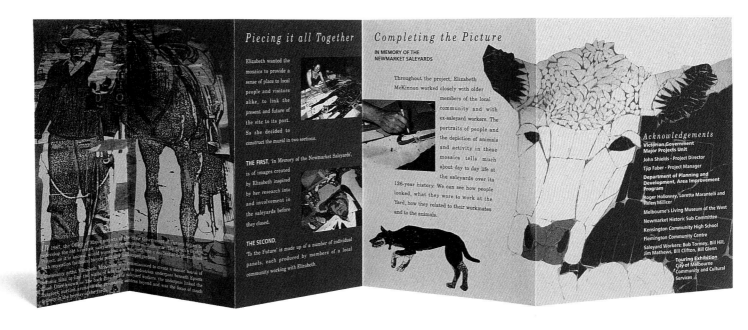

地方自治体　展覧会リーフレット
Local Government　Exhibition Leaflet
Australia　1994

CD, AD, D : **Adele Del Signore**

P : **Colin Boggars**

CW : **Susan Faine**

DF : **In House Design / City of Melbourne**

CL : **Andrew Sea Ward**

SIZE : **200 × 160mm**

デザイン会社　カード製品案内
Design Firm　Holiday Card Brochure
USA　1992

CD, AD, D : **Peat Jariya**

D, P, I : **Spinner**

I : **Fotis**

DF : **Peat Jariya Design**

CW, DF, CL : **[Metal] Studio Corp.**

SIZE : **152 × 204mm**

フランドル政府　デザインプロモーション
Flemish Government　Promotional Leaflet
Belgium　1994

CD, AD, D : **Jo Klaps**

P : **Hans Vos / Kari Decock**

CW : **Johan Valcke**

DF : **Brussels Lof**

CL : **Vizo**

SIZE : **100 × 210mm**

フランドル政府　展覧会案内
Flemish Government　Exhibition Leaflet
Belgium　1995

CD, AD, D : **Jo Klaps / Miet Marneffe**

P : **Eddy Fliers**

DF : **Brussels Lof / De Gelaarsde Kat**

CL : **Vizo**

SIZE : **297 × 100mm**

Page 175
ダンス協会　公演案内
**Dance Organization
Promotional Brochure**
Australia　1994

CD, AD : **Richard Henderson**

D : **Keith Smith**

P : **Jacqui Henshaw**

CW : **Mark Worner**

CL : **Greenmill Dance Project**

SIZE : **298 × 105mm**

BODY KNOWLEDGE AND RELAXATION (AFTER WORK):
WITH THESE SIMPLE EXERCISES AND EXPLORATIONS,
HOLDING IN THE BODY IS RELEASED, ALLOWING REST AND
RECUPERATION TO TAKE PLACE. BASED ON THE
PRINCIPLES OF BODY-MIND CENTRING BY BONNIE
BAINBRIDGE COHEN (USA).

PROFESSIONAL DANCE CLASSES

WITH REBECCA HILTON
THOSE WHO KNOW BECKY HILTON FROM
HER DAYS AT THE VCA SCHOOL OF
DANCE, OR AS A DANCER WITH DANCE
EXCHANGE AND DANCEWORKS WILL
REMEMBER HER AS A PHENOMENAL DANCER, CHARMING
ENTERTAINER AND A GIFTED TEACHER. THIS SUMMER SHE
RETURNS BRIEFLY FROM NEW YORK WHERE SHE
CURRENTLY LIVES AND WORKS AS A DANCER IN THE
STEPHEN PETRONIO COMPANY.
IN A 2-HOUR MORNING TECHNIQUE CLASS, GEARED
TOWARDS PROFESSIONAL AND EXPERIENCED DANCERS,
SHE WILL OFFER AN ECLECTIC MIX THAT COMBINES SOLID
MOVEMENT INFORMATION WITH CHUNKY PHRASES OF
INSPIRED DANCING.
CLASS SIZES LIMITED – SO DON'T MISS OUT!
MONDAY 24 – FRIDAY 28 JANUARY, 9.30-11.30 AM
SINGLE CLASSES $10, CONCESSION $8
WEEKLY $40, $35 CONCESSION
LOWER MELBOURNE TOWN HALL

WITH JIM HUGHES
EASE YOUR BODY INTO GREEN MILL'S
WEEK OF FORUMS BY TAKING A 45-MINUTE
MORNING CLASS, PRESENTED BY
JIM HUGHES, USING THE FELDENKRAIS
METHOD. FELDENKRAIS EXPANDS REPERTOIRES OF
MOVEMENT, FEELING AND EXPRESSION, DEVELOPS
AWARENESS, FLEXIBILITY AND COORDINATION, AND THE
LEARNING OF MORE EFFICIENT, EASIER WAYS OF MOVING.
JIM HUGHES IS ARTISTIC DIRECTOR OF FIELDWORKS
PERFORMANCE GROUP IN PERTH. HE HAS WORKED WITH
THE LINDSAY KEMP MIME COMPANY, DANCED WITH THE
ZURICH OPERA BALLET AND THE GULBENKIAN MODERN
DANCE COMPANY, AND PERFORMED AT THE SYDNEY
BIENNALE. A FORMER LECTURER IN MOVEMENT AND
DANCE AT THE WA ACADEMY OF PERFORMING ARTS,
HE HAS DIRECTED AND CHOREOGRAPHED PRODUCTIONS
FOR FIELDWORKS THAT INCLUDE WHAT THE BODY
REMEMBERS, SCENES IN A PRISON AND TRACES.
TUESDAY 18 – FRIDAY 21 JANUARY, 8-9.45.
$7 PER CLASS, CONCESSION $5
LOWER MELBOURNE TOWN HALL.

12.45 PM THE TRAIL OF CRUMBS 1:
THE CRUMBS OF CAUTION
LOWER MELBOURNE TOWN HALL
THE OPENING SUSPENSEFUL CHAPTER
OF FIVE INTENSELY IMPROVISED
PERFORMANCES BY TROTMAN AND
MORRISH, THE DETECTIVES OF DANCE.

ENTRY INCLUDED IN SEASON AND MINI
TICKETS, OTHERWISE SESSION TICKET
RATES APPLY.

1.15 PM LUNCH

2.30 PM WHAT WAS THAT ALL ABOUT?
HOW DO CHOREOGRAPHERS CREATE
MEANING THROUGH MOVEMENT? HOW CAN
DANCE AUDIENCES READ OR DEVELOP THEIR
UNDERSTANDING OF PERFORMANCES?
PRESENTATION BY HILARY CRAMPTON,
WITH COMMENT FROM MEREDITH
BLACKBURN, TIM STOREY AND JILL SYKES,
CHAIRED BY AMANDA SMITH.

4.30 PM CLASSICAL NARRATIVE:
BALLET AND ITS OFFSHOOTS
ROBIN GROVE ON THE GRECIAN/
APOLLONIAN ORIGINS AND SUBSEQUENT
DEVELOPMENT OF CLASSICAL BALLET, WITH
COMMENT FROM HARRY HAYTHORNE AND
SUE STREET, CHAIRED BY COLIN PEASLEY.

TUESDAY 18 JANUARY

9 AM FELDENKRAIS CLASS
WITH JIM HUGHES
LOWER MELBOURNE TOWN HALL
SEPARATE TICKET REQUIRED. SEE
PROFESSIONAL CLASSES AT BEGINNING
OF BROCHURE.

10 AM CLASSICAL NARRATIVE:
INDIAN AND INDONESIAN
AN HISTORICAL OVERVIEW AND INDICATION
OF CURRENT TRENDS IN CLASSICAL
NARRATIVE FROM PROFESSOR
SOEDARSONO ON INDONESIAN DANCE,
AND TARA RAJKUMAR ON INDIAN DANCE,
CHAIRED BY JOAN GRANT.

Dance

Stretching the Imagination

GREENMILL DANCE PROJECT

MELBOURNE FESTIVAL OF CHOREOGRAPHY & DANCE INC.

16-28 January 1994

GREEN MILL
DANCE PROJECT

7.30-10PM STORY...
THE...
LOWER...
AN...
ST...
T...

9 AM

10

12 PM THE TRAIL...
A SKERRICK OF SCONE...
LOWER MELBOURNE TOWN HALL
IT WASN'T PROFESSOR PLUM OR
MS SCARLETT AND THE CONSERVATORY
WAS OCCUPIED AND YOU HAD THE
SPANNER. WHAT PATH WILL OUR
PROTAGONISTS, TROTMAN AND MORRISH,
PURSUE? ARE THEY MAKING THIS UP?

2 PM DANCE & CULTURAL IDENTITY
PROFESSOR SOEDARSONO, BETH SHELTON,
RAYMOND BLANCO AND RONNIE ARNOLD
DISCUSS DANCE AND CULTURAL IDENTITY,
CHAIRED BY GWENDA BEED DAVEY.

4 PM AUSTRALIA AND THE WORLD
AN INTERNATIONAL PERSPECTIVE ON
AUSTRALIAN DANCE AND NARRATIVE
TRENDS AND THEIR PARALLELS OVERSEAS
FROM DEBORAH JOWITT, AND AN
AUSTRALIAN PERSPECTIVE FROM CLARE
DYSON ON EUROPEAN AND NORTH
AMERICAN DEVELOPMENTS. COMMENT
FROM BECKY HILTON AND NOELLE
SHADER, CHAIRED BY KEITH BAIN.

FRIDAY 21 JANUARY

9 AM FELDENKRAIS CLASS
WITH JIM HUGHES
LOWER MELBOURNE TOWN HALL
SEPARATE TICKET REQUIRED.

10 AM IN THE MOMENT
MARK MICHINTON ON THE STRUCTURES OF
LANGUAGE IN IMPROVISATION AND IN THE
BODY; LLEWELLYN WISHART ON DANCING
THE BODY MAP, A DISCUSSION OF
EXPERIENTIAL ANATOMY AND THE

...MILL DANCE PROJECT
...LL DANCE PROJECT
...2 KAVANAGH STREET
...MELBOURNE VIC 3205
...ALIA
...PHONE (03) 686 8749
...IMILE (03) 686 6186

...OARD
CHAIR ANDREW PORTER
VICE CHAIR NANETTE HASBALL
SECRETARY DON ASKEN
TREASURER CLIVE GREGORY

MARK ANNEAR
MICHAEL BANKS
CARL CARTHY
DESMOND CLARK
HILARY CRAMPTON
VICKI FAIRFAX
MARK GORDON
RICHARD HENDERSON
HELEN HERBERTSON
CASSANDRA JOHNSTONE
GAEL KENNEDY
VIVIAN KNOWLES
SHIRLEY McKECHNIE OAM
JULIAN OLDFIELD
TARA RAJKUMAR
BRYAN SMITH
JONATHAN TAYLOR

OBSERVERS
BUFFY BOWLES
JULIE DYSON
STEPHEN GRANT
DEBRA JEFFERIES
JANET KARIN
JILL RIVERS
CLAIRE STONIER-KIPEN
PROFESSOR GLENN WITHERS

GENERAL MANAGER MARK WOHNER
ADMINISTRATOR BRONWYN JOHNSON
PROJECT MANAGER SANDRA AYACHE
PUBLICITY CONSULTANT JULIE MORGAN
MARKETING & PUBLICITY SERVICES PTY LTD
LEGAL CONSULTANTS NANSCAWEN GRANT
BARRISTERS & SOLICITORS
DESIGN CONSULTANTS FHA DESIGN
AUDITORS KPMG PEAT MARWICK
PHOTOGRAPHY JACQUI HENSHAW

FOR PUBLICITY INFORMATION, CONTACT JULIE MORGAN
ON (03) 525 5688

GREEN MILL
DANCE PROJECT

TICKETS

SEASON TICKET (ALL SESSIONS) $95, CONCESSION $55
MINI TICKET (10 SESSIONS ONLY) $60, CONCESSION $45
SESSION TICKET $7, CONCESSION $5
ADMITTANCE TO LUNCHTIME PERFORMANCES OF THE
TRAIL OF CRUMBS IS INCLUDED IN THE SEASON AND
MINI TICKETS, OTHERWISE SESSION TICKET PRICES APPLY.
PROFESSIONAL DANCE CLASSES: WITH REBECCA HILTON
WEEKLY $40, CONCESSION $35; PER CLASS $10,
CONCESSION $8. WITH JIM HUGHES, PER CLASS $7,
CONCESSION $5.

HOW TO BOOK

1. BY PHONE
RING THE CUB MALTHOUSE BOX OFFICE ON
(03) 685 5111. MOST MAJOR CREDIT CARDS ACCEPTED.
2. BY MAIL
CHEQUES SHOULD BE MADE PAYABLE TO PLAYBOX.
COMPLETE THE BOOKING FORM OVERLEAF AND MAIL WITH
PAYMENT TO:
GREEN MILL BOOKINGS
CUB MALTHOUSE BOX OFFICE
113 STURT STREET
SOUTH MELBOURNE VIC 3205
3. BY FAX
CREDIT CARD BOOKINGS ONLY. COMPLETE THE BOOKING
FORM OVERLEAF AND FAX TO:
GREEN MILL BOOKINGS
CUB MALTHOUSE BOX OFFICE
(03) 685 5112
4. IN PERSON
PRE-BOOK AT THE CUB MALTHOUSE BOX OFFICE,
113 STURT STREET, SOUTH MELBOURNE.
HOURS 9 AM – 5 PM, MONDAY – SATURDAY.
ALSO OPEN SOME EVENINGS UNTIL 8.30 PM, CHECK
ON (03) 685 5111.
TICKETS CAN ALSO BE PURCHASED ON THE DAY AT THE
APPROPRIATE VENUE.

CONCESSIONS
CONCESSION RATES ARE AVAILABLE TO AUSDANCE
MEMBERS, GROUPS OF 10 OR MORE, STUDENTS, THE
UNEMPLOYED AND PENSIONERS. PROOF OF STATUS FOR
ALL CONCESSIONS IS REQUIRED.

CONDITIONS
THERE IS NO REFUND OR EXCHANGE ON COMPLETED
BOOKINGS. ALL PRICES QUOTED INCLUDE BOOKING FEES.
ALL SEATING IS GENERAL ADMISSION. THIS PROGRAM IS
SUBJECT TO CHANGE.

exterior art

Juan Campmany

arte exterior

Juan Campmany

Es muy probable que al recibir un mensaje publicitario desde cualquier soporte de publicidad exterior, no percibamos que dicha comunicación entre emisor y receptor se está produciendo a través del medio más antiguo de los empleados por el hombre para comunicarse.
Es muy probable que no encontremos otro medio que haya contado, y siga contando, con la colaboración de talentos creativos como Picasso, Miró, Casas, Gris, Warhol, Toulouse-Lautrec, Mucha, Cassandre...
Es muy probable que no exista otro medio que ofrezca tantas posibilidades como las que los comunicadores seamos capaces de inventar: pósters, carteles, vallas, murales, luminosos, edificios, estáticos o en movimiento, etc.
La publicidad exterior ha sido el medio que más se ha adaptado a las necesidades de las empresas que desean comunicarse con sus clientes. Ha sido el medio que mejor ha respondido a las demandas de los creativos publicitarios e incluso se ha anticipado a ellas creando futuro.
Hoy en día, con las alternativas que ofrecen otros medios, anunciantes y agencias tienden a considerarlo un medio complementario de otros aparentemente más importantes, olvidando el potencial que tiene como medio principal. Quizás el lector recuerde, al mirar este u otro libro sobre el tema, marcas que se han hecho a sí mismas con este medio.
Roger Velázquez, fotógrafo y creativo, descubre en la publicidad exterior otras facetas: la coincidencia, la grandiosidad, la perspectiva, y nos aclara quizás el porqué del éxito. Porque es arte. Y el arte, afortunadamente, interesa más que la publicidad.
Es muy probable que a la publicidad exterior solo le falte hablar, pero eso, tarde o temprano, también lo veremos.

広告会社　写真展カタログ
Advertising Company
Photo Exhibition Brochure
Spain　1995

CD, P, CW : **Roger Velàzquez**

CD, D, DF : **Gabriel Espi**

CL : **Publivia**

SIZE : **300 × 300mm**

Historisch gesitueerd

13

Philippe **Allaeys**

70

Huub **Berger**

71

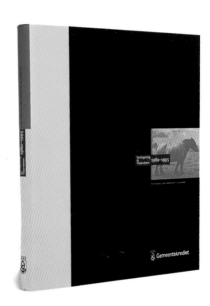

Veerle **Rouquart**

130

Adinda **Saelens**

131

フランドル政府　デザインプロモーション
Flemish Government   Promotional Guidebook
Belgium　1995

CD, AD, D : **Jo Klaps / Miet Marneffe**

P : **Lieven Herreman**

CW : **Johan Valcke / Inge Vranken /
Christian Oosterlinck**

DF : **Brussels Lof / De Gelaarsde Kat**

CL : **Vizo**

SIZE : **300 × 253mm**

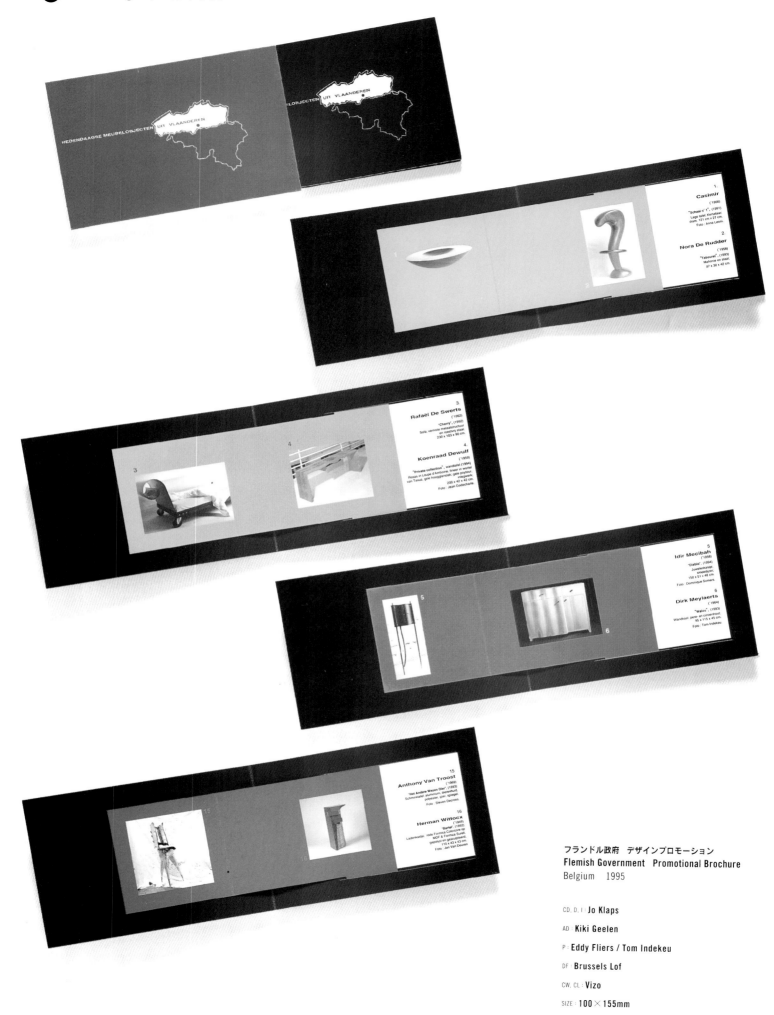

フランドル政府　デザインプロモーション
Flemish Government　Promotional Brochure
Belgium　1995

CD, D, I : **Jo Klaps**

AD : **Kiki Geelen**

P : **Eddy Fliers / Tom Indekeu**

DF : **Brussels Lof**

CW, CL : **Vizo**

SIZE : **100 × 155mm**

A HIGH-FLYING WELCOME
FROM YOUR WOODLAND FRIENDS.

Hi. Did you notice? I'm a flying squirrel. My
wings are hard to see, especially when I've
been packed in a hollow log all winter with
the family.

I consider it quite an honor to be asked to
say a few words on behalf of Summer, who
couldn't make it back early this year. She's on
an ecotour in Costa Rica. I understand it's my
job to evoke her warm and lyrically-beautiful
season, as you'll find it here in these magical,
wooded glens of Spring Green.

Actually, I'm more the thrill seeker type than
the poet. You know, gliding through the air
with the greatest of ease. Maybe you caught
my act last summer, high above the APT stage.
Those of you who didn't think I was a bat!

At any rate, we are looking forward to your
return this summer. You folks sure do light up
our nightlife. And let's face it, what animals
couldn't use a little more fire in that
department, right?

劇場　プロモーション
Outdoor Theatre
Promotional Brochures
USA　1993-1996

CD, AD, D, I, DF : **Planet Design Company**

CW : **John Anderson**

CL : **American Players Theatre**

SIZE : **278 × 140mm**

ギャラリー　展覧会カタログ
Art Gallery　Exhibition Catalogue
Belgium　1996

CD, AD, D : **Jo Klaps / Henk-hans Hilvering**

I, CW : **Johan Clijsters**

DF : **Brussels Lof**

CL : **Chosen With Care**

SIZE : **250 × 176mm**

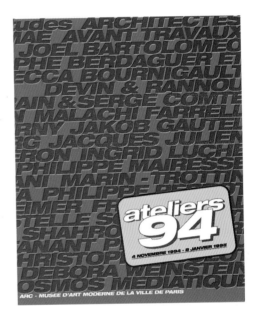

美術館 展覧会カタログ
Museum   Exhibition Brochure
France   1994

CD：Suzanne Koller / Ezra Petronio

P. I：D. R.

DF：Work In Progress

CL：Museum of Modern Art / Paris

SIZE：265 × 205mm

新聞社　ダンス団プロモーション
Newspaper Publisher
Dance Company Promotion
Brasil　1995

CD, AD, D : **Gustavo Portela**

CD : **André de Castro**

DF : **Interface Designers**

CL : **O Globo Newspaper**

SIZE : **280 × 210mm**

Change
Seattle '95

The Sixth National Design Conference
of the American Institute of Graphic Arts
September 28 to October 1, 1995

Design conferences can no longer afford to survive on just portfolio presentations alone. In response to the increased complexities facing our profession, this fall's AIGA Conference in Seattle will galvanize the design community to address issues of scope and importance.

Community

Technology

Come to the world's largest gathering of graphic designers for three extraordinary days in one of America's most exciting cities. You'll join leading entrepreneurs like Smith & Hawken's Paul Hawken and TimeWarner's Walter Isaacson. Leaders in politics and public policy like Senator Bob Kerrey and Samina Quraeshi, NEA Design Program Director. Designers like Erik Spiekermann, Lucille Tenazas, Laurie Haycock Makela, P. Scott Makela, Lorraine Wild, and *Wired*'s Barbara Kuhr & John Plunkett. That's just the beginning…

Opportunity

The Featured Speakers

are leaders from design, government, business, technology and the arts who will tackle the issues that matter.

Janet Abrams	Design journalist and cultural critic
Michael Arent	Project leader, Pacific Telesis Information Systems
Lawrence Barth	Intellectual property law expert
Luanne Cohen	Applications design director, Adobe Systems
Tinker Hatfield	Vice president for special projects, Nike
Paul Hawken	Ecologist and entrepreneur, founder of Smith & Hawken and author of The Next Economy
Walter Isaacson	Editor of New Media, Time Inc.
Senator Bob Kerrey	Nebraska democrat and founder, The New Media Centers Program
Anne Kreamer	Executive vice-president, Creative, Nickelodeon
B. Kuhr & J. Plunkett	Co-founders and creative directors, Wired
Laurie Haycock Makela	Design director, Walker Art Center, Minneapolis
P. Scott Makela	Designer for film, print, and multimedia
Susan Meiselas	Photojournalist and film director
Rebeca Méndez	Design director, Art Center College of Design
Duane Michals	Photographer and writer
Tomoko Miho	Designer and current AIGA Medalist
William J. Mitchell	Dean, MIT School of Architecture and Planning

Seattle '95   The Sixth AIGA NATIONAL DESIGN CONFERENCE

"We need more graphic design particular to the tribes, not less."
Lorraine Wild

"Good design can release humankind from its neurotic relationship to absurd acts of destruction, and aim it toward a destiny that is far more 'realistic' and enduring. The urge to create beauty is an untapped power, and it exists in commerce as well as in society."
Paul Hawken

"If Henry Luce were alive today he'd build a Web site."
Walter Isaacson

"I have an interest in the invisible light, the light perceptible only in the mind. A light which seems to be undimmed by the entering of the senses. I want to address the light that we see in dreams and make spaces that seem to come from those dreams…"
James Turrell

In that great place to visit
you always wanted (or revisit).

If you're sleepless in Seattle, then it's because there's too much to see and do. Seattle is known for its alternative music scene, for giving the old term "coffee house" new meaning, and as home to Microsoft® and the myriad high-technology companies that are reshaping our lives. It's also known for its enviable, outdoor-oriented lifestyle, Pacific Rim-fusion cuisine, and strong commitment to the arts and design. Flanked by the often snow-covered Olympic and Cascade ranges—with Mount Rainier dominating—Seattle occupies an isthmus between Puget Sound and Lake Washington where panoramic mountain, water, and island vistas are inescapable. Points of interest include Seattle Center (location of the 1962 World's Fair, with Pacific Science Center, and the Space Needle), and the splendid Pike Place Farmers' Market. You'll also enjoy visiting the turn-of-the-century Pioneer Square historic district with its clubs and galleries and exploring Capitol Hill's residential architecture. Don't miss a walk to the waterfront along the original "Skid Road" to catch the ferry to Bainbridge Island—an inexpensive, yet glorious way to view the region and its many islands. And after hours, there are places like Dilettante and B&O Espresso where you can have dessert, sip an espresso, and check out what travel writers have called "Seattle's offbeat culture." Sample the local music scene in small bars like Jazz Alley and the Off Ramp. Boating, climbing, and mountain biking are a way of life here, with easily accessible short excursions available (say, on Sunday afternoon after the closing session). Snoqualmie Falls, a great hiking spot, is one of the most frequented attractions in Washington. The temperature ranges from the high forties to the high sixties in September and October. Dress is casual. It drizzles often, so bring a raincoat. But natives don't bother with umbrellas.

270' SNOQUALMIE

MT. Rainier

Falls

デザイン協会　協議会案内
Design Association   Conference Guide
USA   1995

CD, AD, D : **Rick Eiber**
P : **Tony Stone Images**
CW : **Ellen Shapird**
DF : **Rick Eiber Design（Red）**
CL : **American Institute of Graphic Arts**
SIZE : **229×139mm**

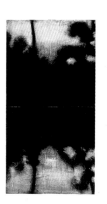

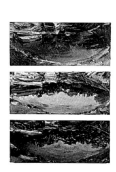

アートセンター　展覧会カタログ
Arts Center　Exhibition Brochure
USA　1995

CD, AD, D : **John Ball**

DF : **Mires Design, Inc.**

CL : **California Center for the Arts Museum**

SIZE : **304 × 164mm**

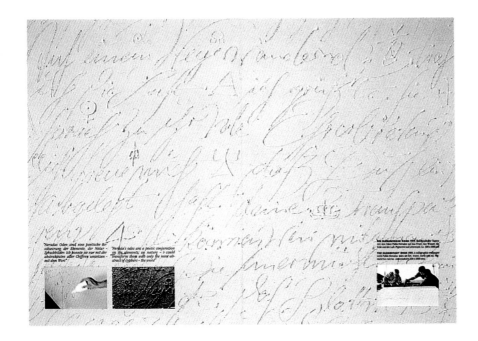

THE PREMINGER ART COLLECTION

飲料メーカー　美術品コレクションカタログ
Brewery　Art Collection Catalogue
Germany　1990

CD, I : **Achim Kiel**

P : **Ute Karen Seggelke née Walter /**

Uwe Brandes

CW : **Paul Barz**

DF : **Pencil Corporate Art**

CL : **Preminger Bierstaette**

SIZE : **309 × 209mm**

ギターメーカー　製品案内
**Guitar Manufacturer
Product Brochure**
USA　1995

CD, AD, D : **Scott Mires**

P : **Chris Wimpey**

DF : **Mires Design, Inc.**

CL : **Taylor Guitars**

SIZE : **110 × 236mm**

ギターメーカー　製品案内
**Guitar Manufacturer
Product Brochure**
USA　1996

CD, AD, D : **Scott Mires**

P : **Chris Wimpey**

DF : **Mires Design, Inc.**

CL : **Taylor Guitars**

SIZE : **280 × 280mm**

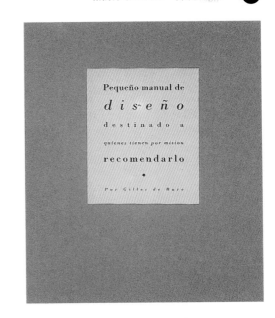

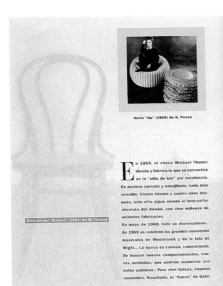

テレビ／ビデオ会社　デザインガイド
TV-Video Company　Design Guide
France　1993

CD, AD : **Alain Lachartre**

CD : **Philippe Starck**

D : **Eudes Bulard**

CW : **Gilles de Bure**

DF : **Vue Sur la Ville**

CL : **Thomson**

SIZE : **209 × 169mm**

放送局　フィルムコレクションカタログ
Broadcasting Company
Film Collection Catalogue
USA　1994

CD, CW : **Alison Hill**

D, I : **Tracy Sabin**

P, I : **Studio Archives**

DF : **Tracy Sabin Graphic Design**

CL : **Turner Broadcasting**

SIZE : **230 × 145mm**

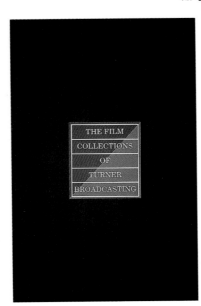

テレビ局　番組紹介
Television Station
Programming Brochure
USA　1995

CD : **Kenna Kay / Laurie Hinzman /**
　　Nick at Nite

AD, D, I : **Melinda Beck**

DF : **Melinda Beck Studio**

CL : **Nick at Nite**

SIZE : **240 × 300mm**

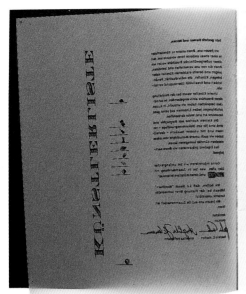

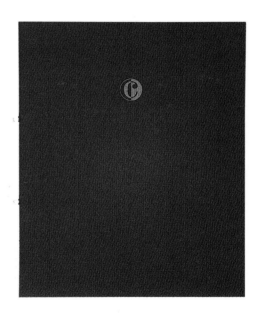

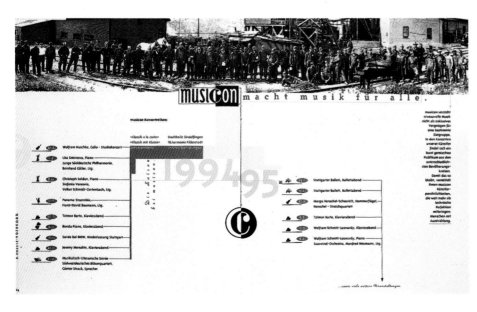

ミュージシャンエージェンシー　プロモーション
Music Artist's Agency　Promotional Brochure
Germany　1994

CD, AD, D : **Jochen Rädeker**

DF : **Strichpunkt / Stuttgart**

CL : **Musicon**

SIZE : **265 × 210mm**

2

Antonio Carlos Jobim, 1927-1994

6

Carmen Santos Ritenour, Producer

Lee Ritenour, Musical Producer

João Gilberto

Sting

"Tom is like a brother. I love his music. His art is the beauty."
—JOAO GILBERTO

inspiration

composer
—STING

16

Jobim Tribute Staff

a tribute to antonio carlos

j. jobim

Avery Fisher Hall, Lincoln Center

April 18th 8:pm
1995

"What was left was the silence of the stones, of the brave plants that grow so slowly, and of the sky and of the earth, in their places."
—JOAO GUIMARÃES ROSA

プロダクション／大使館　コンサートプログラム
Entertainment Company
Concert Promotional Brochure
USA　1995

CD, AD : Petrula Vrontikis

D : Kim Sage

P : Anna Jobim

CW : Carmen Ritenour

DF : Vrontikis Design Office

CL : CS Productions / The Brazilian Embassy

SIZE : 280 × 216mm

映画会社　映画プロモーション
Movie Company　Movie Promotional Brochure
USA　1995

CD, AD, D : Mike Salisbury

D : Patrick O'neal

P : Joel D. Warren / Bruce Birmelow

DF : Mike Salisbury Communications, Inc.

CL : MGM

SIZE : 360 × 280mm

So wha
the winds
a-telling
laddie?

BLOWN
AWAY

Camping Cosmos
de Jan Bucquoy

Black Dju

Transatlantic Films

Communauté Française de Belgique · DGCC · Direction de l'Audiovisuel · Centre du Cinéma et de l'Audiovisuel

Un été
à La Goulette
de Férid Boughedir

Un divan à New York

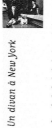

de long
en large

Lamy Films

Eric Lagesse
FPI - Flach Pyramide
International

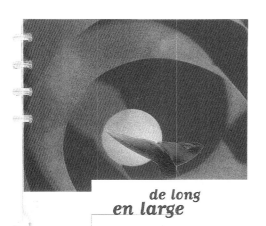

Les aveux
de l'innocent
de Jean-Pierre Améris

William Z.

Sophimages

Cinesport

芸術振興団体　映画プロモーション
Ministry of Arts　Film Promotional Brochure
Belgium　1995

CD, AD : **Sébastien Houtart**

AD, D : **Katrien Florin**

DF : **Signé Lazer**

CL : **French Community of Belgium**

SIZE : **285 × 202mm**

PRESSESTIMMEN ZU KEN FOLLETT
und seinen Büchern

EIN PORTRAIT DES AUTORS
von Siegfried Aelt

BUCHBESPRECHUNG　KEN FOLLETT　DIE PFEILER DER MACHT

KEN FOLLETT

DIE PFEILER DER MACHT
ROMAN LÜBBE

BÜCHER, DIE BLEIBEN
Die Buchkunst des Achim Kiel

出版社　新刊案内
Publisher　Promotional Brochure
Germany　1994

CD : Barbara Fischer / Arno Haering

AD. I : Achim Kiel

P : Ute Karen Seggelke / Lutz Pape / Jutta Bruedern /
Uwe Brandes / Gudrun Stoeckinger

DF : Pencil Corporate Art

CL : Gustav Luebbe Verlag

SIZE : 309 × 209mm

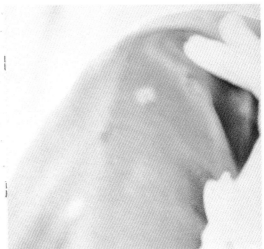

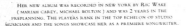

HER NEW ALBUM WAS RECORDED IN NEW YORK BY RIC WAKE
(MARIAH CAREY, MICHAEL BOLTON) AND WAS 2 YEARS IN THE
PREPLANNING. THE PLAYERS RANK IN THE TOP ECHELON OF STUDIO
MUSICIANS AND THE SONGS SHOWCASE HER AS A PREMIERE SONGWRITER.

ON OCTOBER 25TH, 1991
YOU WON'T BELIEVE YOUR EARS.

THE VOICE THAT NEEDS NO INTRODUCTION.

KATHY TROCCOLI

レコード会社　プロモーション
Record Company　Product Introduction
USA　1990

CD : Stan Evenson

DF : Evenson Design Group

CL : Reunion Records

SIZE : 203 × 203mm

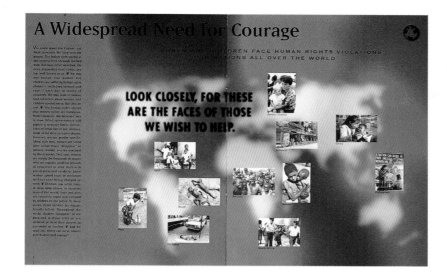

人権擁護団体　プロモーション
Non-Profit Organization　Fund Raising Brochure
USA　1995

CD, AD, D, I : **Mark Bult**

CD, CW : **Holly Kaslewicz**

P : **Jason L. Ables（Cover）**

DF : **Western Front Graphics**

CL : **Amnesty International USA /
The Ginetta Sagan Fund**

SIZE : **279 × 228mm**

非営利団体　キャンプ案内
Non-Profit Association　Camp Information
USA　1993

CD, AD, D : **George S. Moy**

D : **Kimberly Hohenberger**

P : **Mark Packo**

CW : **Patricia Sierra**

DF : **Summit Communications, Inc.**

CL : **YMCA Storer Camp**

SIZE : **280 × 215mm**

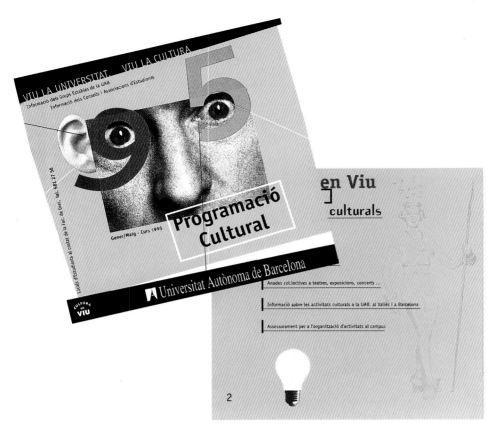

大学　講座案内
University Cultural Program Guide
Spain　1995

CD, AD : **Ramon Enrich**

CD, D : **Lluis Jubert**

P : **Arxive Espai Grafic**

CW, DF : **Espai Grafic**

CL : **Universitat Autònoma de Barcelona**

SIZE : **220 × 230mm**

WISCONSIN'S LAST GREAT PLACES

DIVISION 1
Lake Superior Lowland: Boreal Forest

This division lies between Lake Superior and the highland to the south. Most of the lowland is undulating to rolling plain with some level and hilly areas. In presettlement time, about 83% of the Lake Superior Lowland was covered by boreal forest of white spruce, balsam fir, white cedar, and paper birch. Red and white pine stands and northern mesic forest of hemlock, yellow birch, and sugar maple occupied the remaining area.

DIVISION 2
Northern Wisconsin Highland: Deciduous & Coniferous Forest

This largest division of Wisconsin's land area spans the state from the Mississippi River in high points such as Timm's Hill, a collapsed hummock in Price County, and Sugar Bush Hill on a moraine in Forest County. The presettlement vegetation was northern mesic forest of sugar maple, yellow birch, and hemlock interspersed with extensive stands of white and red pine and second pine barrens of jack pine and Hill's oak. Numerous peat bogs supported black spruce, tamarack, and white cedar.

DIVISION 3
Lake Michigan Shoreland: Northern Deciduous Forest & Conifer Forest

The forest of this division contains American beech, a species of the eastern deciduous forest that reaches its western limits in extreme eastern parts of Wisconsin. The division ranges in elevation from 580 feet at Lake Michigan to about 1,000 feet on moraines 20 miles west of Green Bay. In addition to beech, the native forests in this division include sugar maple, basswood, yellow birch, elm and hemlock. Wetland communities were once interspersed throughout the division.

DIVISION 4
Central Plains: Oak-Pine Barrens, Oak Forest, Oak Savanna, & Wetlands

This division varies in elevation from 803 feet at Black River Falls on the west to about 1,200 feet at Sheep Pasture Bluff on the north. This western portion is unglaciated lake plain, nearly level, with numerous sandstone buttes and rolling moraine. The presettlement vegetation included oak savanna, pine-oak barrens, and extensive wetland communities.

DIVISION 5
Southeastern Wisconsin Ridges & Lowlands: Deciduous Forest, Savanna, & Prairie

Elevation in this division ranges from 580 feet at Lake Michigan to 1,335 feet on Holy Hill, atop the Kettle Moraine where it overlies the Niagaran escarpment. The division is characterized on the east by a series of moraine ridges, paralleling Lake Michigan, including the Kettle Moraine. The south features extensive glacio-lacustrine deposits. Ground moraine and a drumlin field occupy the central section. The native vegetation included deciduous forest, oak savanna, prairie, and wetlands.

DIVISION 6
Southwestern Upland: Deciduous Forest, Oak Savanna, & Prairie

This division has a total relief of 1,124 feet, from 335 feet at the Mississippi River on the southwest to 1,719 feet on Blue Mounds. Much of the hill country is highly dissected by river valleys (coulees), with no evidence of glaciation. The native vegetation includes oak savanna, southern deciduous forest, pine stands of prairie, and extensive river bottom forest. The Driftless Area served as a refuge for endangered northern monkshood and other preglacial, relict plant species found there, but absent from glaciated areas of the state.

Source: Wisconsin Department of Natural Resources

Located in the southeastern portion of the state, the Lulu Lake Preserve stretches into both Walworth and

Waukesha counties. A high-quality wetland ecosystem, the preserve encompasses the upper reaches of the Mukwonago River. Declared a State Natural Area, the preserve is considered to be of significant scientific interest.

LULU LAKE

"These Wisconsin oak openings were a common paradise for song birds, and a fine place for me to get acquainted with them."
- John Muir -

Located in the vast Kettle Moraine region, Lulu Lake boasts some of the highest quality water in Wisconsin. Its waters, along with the Mukwonago River, protect the highest number of rare fish species in the state.

The preserve houses 59 of the 159 species of fish in Wisconsin, including a few that are glacial relict species. Additionally, the surrounding areas contain numerous rare plants, including Ohio goldenrod, bog anemone grass, and grass of Parnassus. The southern kitten tail, rarely seen outside of this region, flourishes on preserve grounds in over 100 locations.

The preserve also contains rare oak openings, where widely scattered oak trees provide unique sanctuary for an assortment of species. Over fifty acres of this globally scarce natural community are still

found at Lulu Lake and are among the best remaining examples of this resource in the world.

Few ecosystems are as precious as wetlands, and those at this preserve are model examples of their important role in nature.

These efficient natural water-management systems cleanse polluted waters, prevent and moderate flooding, protect shorelines, and recharge ground aquifers.

Water Lily

Lulu Lake

THE BLANDING'S TURTLE

Even when an area of land is purchased and protected, there is no guarantee that every species will be safeguarded from the impact of the outside world.

One of the many threatened species that resides at Lulu Lake is the Blanding's turtle. Volunteers for The Nature Conservancy have been recording information about their population and their activities in the area with great interest and concern.

By examining their shell, it is possible to determine the age of a Blanding's turtle up until its twentieth year. Only one juvenile turtle has been spotted at Lulu Lake in the last three years.

This indicates that although Blanding's turtles are still present at Lulu Lake, their population may be decreasing. Future research will concentrate on strategies to encourage successful propagation and a stable population by locating and protecting their nesting sites and studying their use of the area. We can help make Lulu Lake a permanent home for Blanding's turtles.

THE CAMPAIGN FOR
WISCONSIN'S LAST GREAT PLACES

The Nature Conservancy

CAPITAL CAMPAIGN ALLOCATIONS

The funds raised in the course of the capital campaign will be allocated to five primary areas. The costs for one these five capital campaign will totalic less than 3% of the total revenue generated.

ECOSYSTEM CONSERVATION - $9,300,000
Funds allocated to Ecosystem Conservation will finance the complex activities required to protect large landscapes. They will be used to actually acquire selected properties. They will be used to help coordinate the development of appropriate land practices among private and corporate landowners and various public agencies. This effort will involve educating and working with numerous individuals and organizations.

NEW PRESERVE ACQUISITION - $5,000,000
A portion of the capital campaign funds will be used for the traditional Nature Conservancy approach of land acquisition. These funds will be used to help complete needed land acquisition in key on-going longer term projects, such as the Chiwaukee Prairie, Spring Green Preserve and Quincy Bluff and Wetlands.

SCIENCE & STEWARDSHIP - $2,600,000
Ongoing support is needed to ensure that we continue our important scientific research efforts throughout the State of Wisconsin. Building and maintaining science-based partnerships to improve and update current ecosystem inventories will require significant staff resources. Land stewardship will ensure that land currently under protection is managed in a way that maximizes the value of the habitat for the future. Although operational funding is normally raised during our annual membership drive, in order to prepare for these contingencies we want to raise the equivalent of one year's operating expense as part of this capital campaign.

INTERNATIONAL HABITAT CONSERVATION - $500,000
Wisconsin is the summer nesting ground for a large number of birds that winter in Mexico and Central and South America. Protecting these valuable species involves an international perspective. The Nature Conservancy of Wisconsin is teaming up with both indigenous peoples and public conservation agencies in our sister state of Nicaragua to protect important rainforest habitat at the BOSAWAS Reserve.

CONSERVATION ACTION FUND - $600,000
Given the rapid change in the environmental climate and the pressing manner in which many new projects arrive at our offices, we often need to be quick to react to new tomorrows. We cannot always anticipate this need for immediate action in our annual plans and budgets.

Wisconsin is blessed with an abundance of natural riches. Our children deserve to know them. In at least have the opportunity.

We have a vision that will bridge today with tomorrow. One that honors community and respects the symbiosis of relationships, within wildcare ecosystem and between economic and ecologic considerations. A vision of the interrelationships of our species and this nurturing planet.

The Nature Conservancy is taking bold steps in important places like The Baraboo Hills, the Door Peninsula, Kakagon Sloughs and Lulu Lake--steps that will mark the beginning of a new era for conservation in the Midwest.

But we need your help.

Please join our efforts to protect
WISCONSIN'S LAST GREAT PLACES.
So easy to take for granted.
So difficult to imagine living without.

環境保護団体　プロモーション
**Environmental Protection Group
Fund Raising Brochure**
USA　1995

CD, D : **Jane Jenkins / Tom Jenkins**

CW : **Jim Thackray**

DF : **The Design Foundry**

CL : **The Nature Conservancy**

SIZE : **280 × 215mm**

seafood harvest

1995
exhibitors information

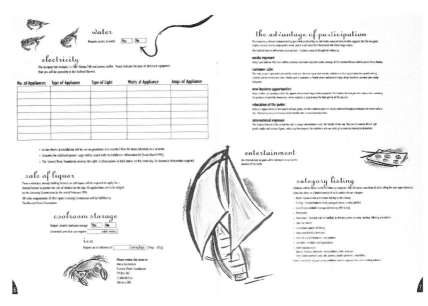

地方自治体　イベント参加者用案内
Local Government　Exhibitors Information
Australia　1994

CD, AD, D : **Sean Savanah**

I : **Rosanna Vecchio**

DF : **In House Design / City of Melbourne**

CL : **Seafood Harvest Comittee / City of Melbourne**

SIZE : **297 × 210mm**

地方観光局　プロモーション
Local Tourism Office　Promotional Brochure
Italy　1993

CD, AD, D, P, CW : **Giona Maiarelli**

CD, AD, D, P : **Ann Rathkopf**

P : **Luciano Morotti**

DF : **Maiarelli & Rathkopf**

CL : **Provincia di Bologna**

SIZE : **290 × 150mm**

SUVIANA
BEACH

GIOCHI E SPORT SUL LAGO DI SUVIANA

Camugnano

地方自治体　ガイドブック
Local Government　Guide for City Uses
Australia　1994

CD, AD, D : **Adele Del Signore**

P : **Andrew Curtis / Jan Gehl**

DF : **In House Design / City of Melbourne**

P, CL : **Nathan Alexander**

SIZE : **210 × 297mm**

Encouraging more people to use the city

DEFINING A LIVEABLE CITY

Stationary activities

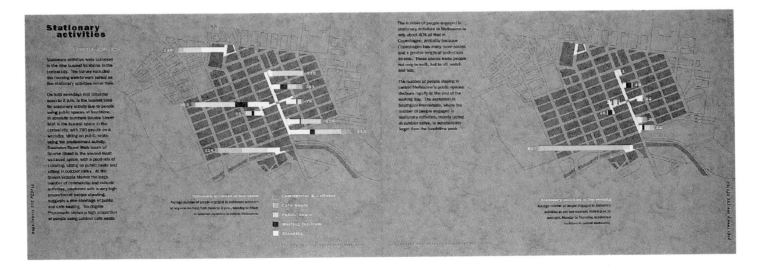

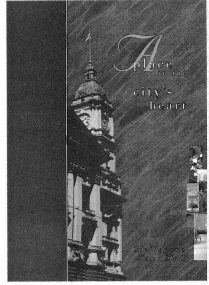

地方自治体　プロモーション
Local Government　Promotional Brochure

Australia　1994

CD, AD : **Adele Del Signore / Angela Panettieri**

D : **Nicholas Mau**

P : **Ponch Hawkes**

DF : **In House Design / City of Melbourne**

CL : **Mark Drew**

SIZE : **320 × 225mm**

地方自治体　プロモーション
Local Government　Promotional Brochure
Australia　1994

CD, AD, D : **Sean Savanah**

P : **Andrew Curtis**

DF : **In House Design**

CL : **Shire of Melton**

SIZE : **594 × 420mm**

家族教育団体　イベント案内
Family-Education Organization　Event Guides
Austria　1991-1993

CD, AD, D, I, CW：**Peter Felder**

P：**Nikolaus Walter**

CW：**Cornelia Drechsel**

DF：**Felder Grafik Design**

CL：**Amt der Vorarlberger Landesregierung**

　　（**Familienreferat**）

SIZE：**210×130mm**

市立劇場　フェスティバルプロモーション
City Hall　Festival Promotion
Spain　1994

CD, AD : Ramon Enrich

CD, D : Lluis Jubert

CW, DF : Espai Grafic

CL : Ajuntament D'igualada

SIZE : 310 × 160mm

市役所　ファッションプロモーション
City Office　Fashion Promotion
Canada　1991

CD : **Ghyslaine Fallu**

AD : **Martin Beauvais**

D, DF : **Tam-Tam Inc.**

P : **Carl Lessard / Barry Harris /
Sofie Richard / Linda Corbett**

I : **Louise Savoie**

CL : **Ville de Montreál**

SIZE : **418 × 284mm**

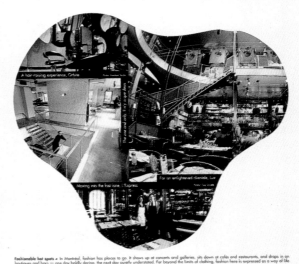

レーシングカー団体　プロモーション
Racing Car Group　Promotional Brochure
USA　1995

AD, D : Jack Anderson

D : Julie Lock / Alan Florsheim

CW : Team Scandia

DF : Hornall Anderson Design Works, Inc.

CL : Scandia

SIZE : 317×228mm

1. ガス会社　ガス節約案内
Gas Company
Gas Conservation Guide
USA　1992

CD, AD, D : **Julia Chong Tam**

I : **Raphael Lopez**

DF : **Julia Tam Design**

CL : **Southern California**
　　Gas Company

SIZE : **204 × 204mm**

2. ガス会社　使用説明書
Gas Company
Product Brochure
USA　1993

CD, AD, D : **Julia Chong Tam**

I : **Mercedes McDonald**

CW : **Peter Brown**

DF : **Julia Tam Design**

CL : **Southern California**
　　Gas Company

SIZE : **240 × 148mm**

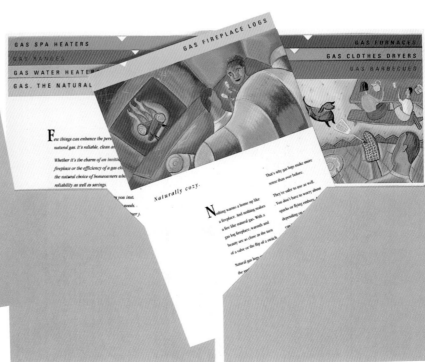

通信販売会社　商品案内
Mail Order Company　Product Brochure
The Netherlands　1992

CD, AD, D, DF : **Corien Bos**

P : **Bas Wilders / Edland Man /**
Felice Derkinderen / Angele Etoundi Essamba

CL : **Mail & Female**

SIZE : **277 × 219mm**

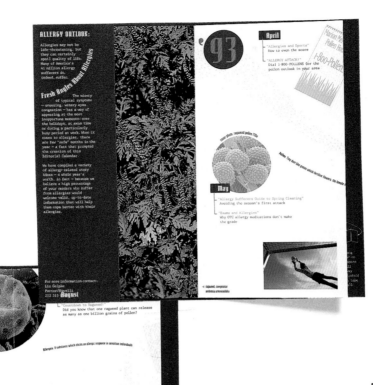

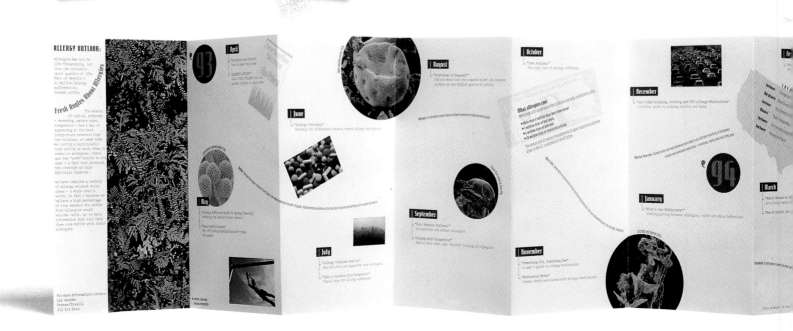

製薬会社　アレルギーカレンダー
Pharmaceutical Company　Editorial Calendar
USA　1993

CD, AD, D : **Sergio Steuer**

CW : **Liz Gelpke**

DF : **Porter / Novelli**

CL : **Marion Merrel Dow Inc.**

SIZE : **236×133mm**

ガス会社　ガス節約のためのアンケート
Gas Company　Promotional Survey
USA　1995

CD, AD, D : Julia Chong Tam
 : Carol O'malia
DF : Julia Tam Design
CL : Southern California Gas Company
SIZE : 277 × 190mm

種子会社　プロモーション
Seedling Exporter　Promotional Brochure
Australia　1994

AD, D, I : **Annette Harcus**

D : **Lucy Walker**

P : **Richard Bennett / Mike Langford /
Brad Miller / Stephen Frink**

I : **Mario Milostic / Louis Allach / Melinda Dudley**

CW : **Jane Caro**

DF : **Harcus Design**

CL : **Lord Howe Island Board**

SIZE : **210×297 mm**

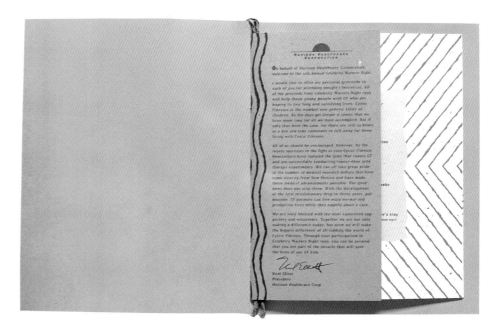

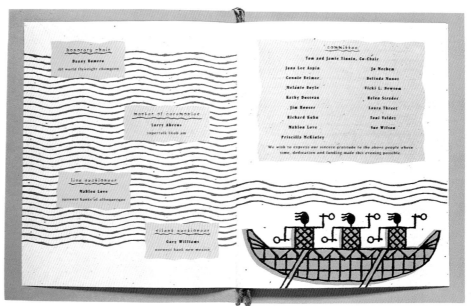

ヘルスケアサービス会社　チャリティプログラム
Healthcare Provider
Charity Program Brochure
USA　1995

CD, AD, D, I : **Rick Vaughn**

CW : **Richard Kuhn**

DF : **Vaughn Wedeen Creative**

CL : **Horizon Healthcare**

SIZE : **253 × 191mm**

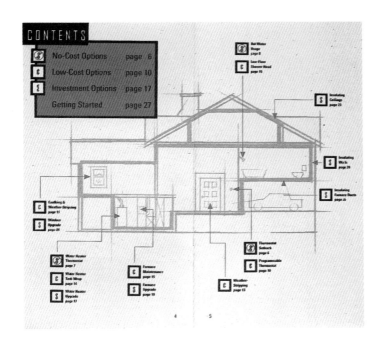

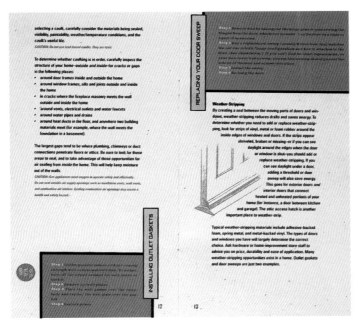

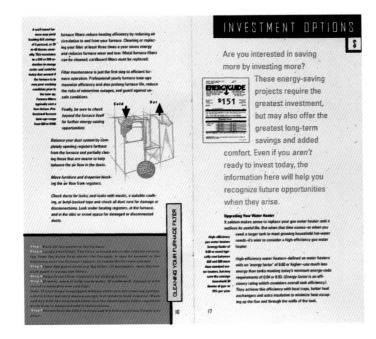

ガス会社　ガス節約案内
Gas Company　Promotional Brochure
USA　1995

CD：**Ken Widmeyer**

AD, D：**Dale Hart**

I：**Tony Secolo**

CW：**Scott Forslund / Kellie Kuhlman**

DF：**Widmeyer Design**

CL：**Washington Natural Gas**

SIZE：**274 × 146mm**

ディスコ　プロモーション
Disco　Promotional Brochure
Italy　1993

CD. AD : **Ennio Zangheri**

D. : **Giuliano Gasperoni**

P. : **Mario Ventimiglia**

CW. : **Loretta Montironi**

DF : **B & AR Communication S. R. L.**

CL : **Paradiso Club**

SIZE : **400 × 300mm**

1

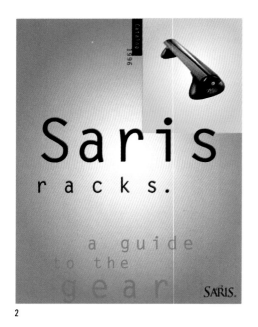

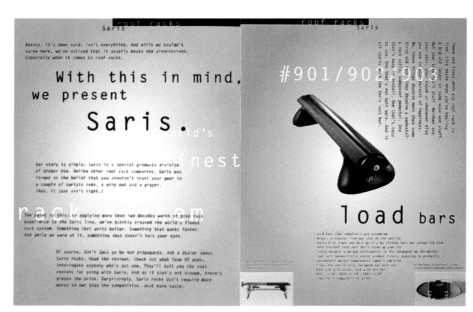

2

1. マグネットメーカー　プロモーション　Magnet Supplier　Promotional Brochure　UK　1992
D：Richard Whitmore　DF：Checkland Kindleysides　CL：Magnet Trade　SIZE：314×314mm（Cover）/ 209×209mm（Brochure）

2. ラックメーカー　製品案内　Rack Manufacturer　Promotional Brochure　USA　1996
CD, AD, D, I, CW, DF：Planet Design Company　P：Sutter Photography / Mark Salisbury Studios　CL：Gräber USA　SIZE：280×216mm

Index

Index of clients

Index of submittors

brochure design forum

Art Director

Douglas Gordon

Designer

Tomoko Sekine

Editor

Kaoru Endo

Photographer

Kuniharu Fujimoto

English Translator

Sue Herbert

Publisher

Shingo Miyoshi

Special Thanks to

Thomas Ballatore

Yutaka Hasegawa

1997年2月7日　初版第1版発行

発行所　ピエ・ブックス

〒170 東京都豊島区駒込4-14-6-301
編集 TEL: 03-3949-5010 FAX: 03-3949-5650
営業 TEL: 03-3940-8302 FAX: 03-3576-7361

© 1997 PIE BOOKS

Printed in Singapore

ISBN4-89444-034-2 C3070

brochure design forum

P·I·E Books

An International Collection of Brochures, Pamphlets and Catalogues

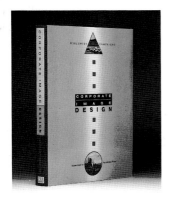

CORPORATE IMAGE DESIGN
世界の業種別ＣＩ・ロゴマーク
Pages: 336 (272 in Color) ￥16,000
An effective logo is the key to brand or company recognition. This sourcebook of total CI design introduces pieces created for a wide range of businesses - from boutiques to multinationals - and features hundreds of design concepts and applications.

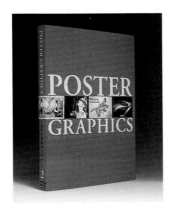

POSTER GRAPHICS Vol. 2
好評！業種別世界のポスター集大成、第２弾
Pages: 256 (192 in Color) ￥17,000
700 posters from the top creators in Japan and abroad are showcased in this book - classified by business. This invaluable reference makes it easy to compare design trends among various industries and corporations.

BROCHURE & PAMPHLET COLLECTION Vol. 4
好評！業種別カタログ・コレクション、第４弾
Pages: 224 (Full Color) ￥16,000
The fourth volume in our popular "Brochure & Pamphlet" series. Twelve types of businesses are represented through artwork that really sells. This book conveys a sense of what's happening right now in the catalog design scene. A must for all creators.

BROCHURE DESIGN FORUM Vol. 2
世界の最新カタログ・コレクション
Pages: 224 (176 in Color) ￥16,000
A special edition of our "Brochure & Pamphlet Collection" featuring 250 choice pieces that represent 70 types of businesses and are classified by business for handy reference. A compendium of the design scene at a glance.

A CATALOGUE AND PAMPHLET COLLECTION
業種別商品カタログ特集／ソフトカバー
Pages: 224 (Full Color) ￥3,800
A collection of the world's most outstanding brochures,catalogs and leaflets classified by industry such as fashion, restaurants, music, interiors and sports goods.Presenting each piece in detail from cover to inside. This title is an indispensable sourcebook for all graphic designers and CI professionals.

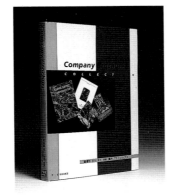

COMPANY BROCHURE COLLECTION
業種別（会社・学校・施設）案内グラフィックス
Pages: 224 (192 in Color) ￥16,000
A rare selection of brochures and catalogs ranging from admission manuals for colleges and universities, to amusement facility and hotel guidebooks, to corporate and organization profiles. The entries are classified by industry for easy reference.

COMPANY BROCHURE COLLECTION Vol. 2
業種別会社案内グラフィックス　第２弾！
Pages: 224 (Full Color) ￥16,000
Showing imaginative layouts that present information clearly in limited space,and design that effectively enhances corporate identity,this volume will prove to be an essential source book for graphic design work of the future.

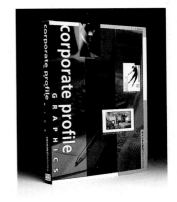

CORPORATE PROFILE GRAPHICS
世界の会社案内グラフィックス
Pages: 224 (Full Color) ￥16,000
A new version of our popular "Brochure and Pamphlet Collection" series featuring 200 carefully selected catalogs from around the world. A substantial variety of school brochures, company profiles and facility information is offered.

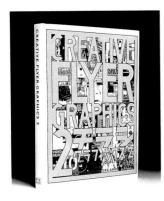

CREATIVE FLYER GRAPHICS Vol. 2
世界のフライヤーデザイン傑作選
Pages: 224 (Full Color) ￥16,000
A pack of some 600 flyers and leaflets incorporating information from a variety of events including exhibitions, movies, plays, concerts, live entertainment and club events, as well as foods, cosmetics, electrical merchandise and travel packages.

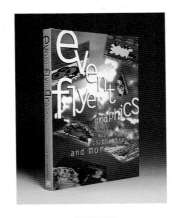

EVENT FLYER GRAPHICS
世界のイベントフライヤー・コレクション
Pages: 224 (Full Color) ￥16,000
Here's a special selection zooming in on flyers promoting events. This upbeat selection covers wide-ranging music events,as well as movies,exhibitions and the performing arts.

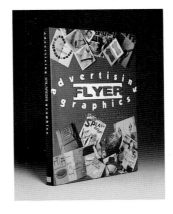

ADVERTISING FLYER GRAPHICS
衣・食・住・遊の商品チラシ特集
Pages: 224 (Full Color) ￥16,000
The eye-catching flyers selected for this new collection represent a broad spectrum of businesses,and are presented in a loose classification covering four essential areas of modern lifestyles: fashion,dining,home and leisure.

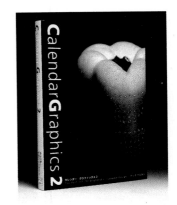

CALENDAR GRAPHICS Vol. 2
好評カレンダー・デザイン集の決定版、第２弾
Pages: 224 (192 in Color) ￥16,000
The second volume of our popular "Calendar Graphics" features designs from about 250 1994 and 1995 calendars from around the world. A rare collection including those on the market as well as exclusive corporate PR calendars.

DIAGRAM GRAPHICS Vol. 2
世界のダイアグラム・デザインの集大成
Pages: 224 (192 in Color)　￥16,000
The unsurpassed second volume in our "Diagram Graphics" series is now complete, thanks to cooperation from artists around the world. It features graphs, charts and maps created for various media.

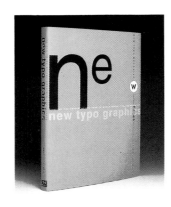

NEW TYPO GRAPHICS
世界の最新タイポグラフィ・コレクション
Pages: 224 (192 in Color)　￥16,000
Uncompromising in its approach to typographic design, this collection includes 350 samples of only the very finest works available. This special collection is a compendium of all that is exciting along the leading edge of typographic creativity today.

1, 2 & 3 COLOR GRAPHICS
1・2・3色グラフィックス
Pages: 208 (Full Color)　￥16,000
Featured here are outstanding graphics in limited colors. See about 300 samples of 1,2 & 3-color artwork that are so expressive they often surpass the impact of full four-color reproductions. This is a very important book that will expand the possibilities of your design work in the future.

1, 2 & 3 COLOR GRAPHICS Vol. 2
1・2・3色グラフィックス、第2弾
Pages: 224 (Full Color)　￥16,000
Even more ambitious in scale than the first volume, this second collection of graphics displays the unique talents of graphic designers who work with limited colors. An essential reference guide to effective, low-cost designing.

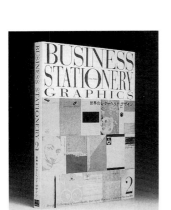

BUSINESS STATIONERY GRAPHICS Vol. 2
世界のレターヘッド・コレクション、第2弾
Pages: 224 (176 in Color)　￥16,000
The second volume in our popular "Business Stationery Graphics" series. This publication focuses on letterheads, envelopes and business cards, all classified by business. Our collection will serve artists and business people well.

BUSINESS CARD GRAPHICS Vol. 1 / Soft Jacket
世界の名刺コレクション／ソフトカバー
Pages: 224 (160 in Color)　￥3,800
First impressions of an individual or company are often shaped by their business cards. The 1,200 corporate and personal-use business cards shown here illustrate the design strategies of 500 top Japanese, American and European designers. PIE's most popular book.

NEW BUSINESS CARD GRAPHICS
最新版！ビジネスカード　グラフィックス
Pages: 224(Full Color)　￥16,000
A selection of 900 samples representing the works of top designers worldwide. Covering the broadest spectrum of business categories, this selection of the world's best business cards ranges from the trendiest to the most classy and includes highly original examples along the way.

BUSINESS PUBLICATION GRAPHICS
業種別企業ＰＲ誌・フリーペーパーの集大成！
Pages: 224 (Full Color)　￥16,000
This comprehensive graphic book introduces business publications created for a variety of business needs, including promotions from boutiques and department stores, exclusive clubs, local communities and company newsletters.

POSTCARD GRAPHICS Vol. 4
世界の業種別ポストカード・コレクション
Pages: 224 (192 in Color)　￥16,000
Our popular "Postcard Graphics" series has been revamped for "Postcard Graphics Vol. 4." This first volume of the new version showcases approximately 1,000 pieces ranging from direct mailers to private greeting cards, selected from the best around the world.

POSTCARD COLLECTION Vol. 2
ポストカードコレクション／ソフトカバー
Pages: 230 (Full Color)　￥3,800
Welcome to the colorful world of postcards with 1200 postcards created by artists from all over the world classified according to the business of the client.

TRAVEL & LEISURE GRAPHICS
ホテル＆旅行 案内 グラフィックス
Pages: 224 (Full Color)　￥16,000
A giant collection of some 400 pamphlets, posters and direct mailings exclusively delivered for hotels, inns, resort tours and amusement facilities.

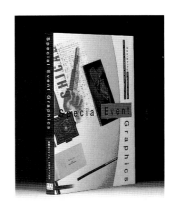

SPECIAL EVENT GRAPHICS
世界のイベント・グラフィックス
Pages: 224 (192 in Color)　￥16,000
A showcase for event graphics, introducing leaflets for exhibitions, fashion shows, all sorts of sales promotional campaigns, posters, premiums and actual installation scenes from events around the world. An invaluable and inspirational resource book, unique in the world of graphic publishing.

3-D GRAPHICS
3Dグラフィックスの大百科
Pages: 224 (192 in Color)　¥16,000
350 works that demonstrate some of the finest examples of 3-D graphic methods, including DMs, catalogs, posters, POPs and more. The volume is a virtual encyclopedia of 3-D graphics.

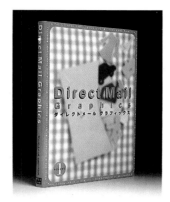

PROMOTIONAL GREETING CARDS
ADVERTISING GREETING CARDS Vol. 4
(English Title)
厳選された世界の案内状＆DM
Pages: 224 (Full Color)　¥16,000
A total of 500 examples of cards from designers around the world. A whole spectrum of stylish and inspirational cards, are classified by function for easy reference.

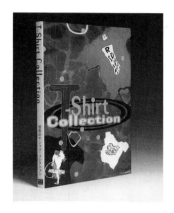

DIRECT MAIL GRAPHICS Vol. 1
衣・食・住のセールスDM特集
Pages: 224 (Full Color)　¥16,000
The long-awaited design collection featuring direct mailers with outstanding sales impact and quality design. 350 of the best pieces, classified into 100 business categories.
A veritable textbook of current direct-marketing design.

DIRECT MAIL GRAPHICS Vol. 2
好評！衣・食・住のセールスDM特集！第2弾
Pages: 224 (Full Color)　¥16,000
The second volume in our extremely popular "Direct Mail Graphics" series features a whole range of direct mailers for various purposes; from commercial announcements to seasonal greetings and are also classified by industry.

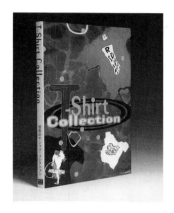

T-SHIRT GRAPHICS / Soft Jacket
世界のTシャツ・コレクション／ソフトカバー
Pages: 224 (192 in Color)　¥3,800
This stunning showcase publication features about 700 T-shirts collected from the major international design centers. Includes various promotional shirts and fabulous designs from the fashion world and sporting-goods manufacturers as well. This eagerly awaited publication has arrived at just the right time.

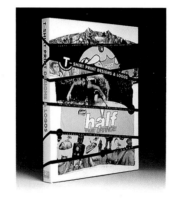

T-SHIRT PRINT DESIGNS & LOGOS
世界のTシャツ・プリント デザイン＆ロゴ
Pages: 224 (192 in Color)　¥16,000
Second volume of our popular "T-shirt Graphics" series. In this publication, 800 designs for T-shirt graphics, including many trademarks and logotypes are showcased. The world's top designers in the field are featured.

The Paris Collections / INVITATION CARDS
パリ・コレクションの招待状グラフィックス
Pages: 176 (Full Color)　¥13,800
This book features 400 announcements for and invitations to the Paris Collections, produced by the world's top names in fashion over the past 10 years. A treasure trove of ideas and pure fun to browse through.

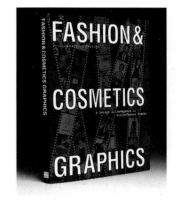

FASHION & COSMETICS GRAPHICS
ファッション＆コスメティック・グラフィックス
Pages: 208 (Full Color)　¥16,000
A collection of promotional graphics from around the world produced for apparel, accessory and cosmetic brands at the avant-garde of the fashion industry. 40 brands featured in this book point the way toward future trends in advertising.

SPORTS GRAPHICS / Soft Jacket
世界のスポーツグッズ・コレクション／ソフトカバー
Pages: 224 (192 in Color)　¥3,800
A collection of 1,000 bold sporting-goods graphic works from all over the world. A wide variety of goods are shown, including uniforms, bags, shoes and other gear. Covers all sorts of sports: basketball, skiing, surfing and many, many more.

LABELS AND TAGS COLLECTION Vol. 1 / Soft Jaket
ラベル＆タグ・コレクション／ソフトカバー
Pages: 224 (192 in Color)　¥3,800
Nowhere is brand recognition more important than in Japan. Here is a collection of 1,600 labels and tags from Japan's 450 top fashion names with page after page of women's and men's clothing and sportswear designs.

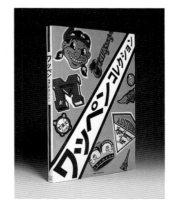

INSIGNIA COLLECTION
ワッペン＆エンブレム・コレクション／ソフトカバー
Pages: 224 (Full Color)　¥3,800
Over 3000 designs were scrutinized for this collection of 1000 outstanding emblems and embroidered motifs that are visually exciting, make innovative use of materials and compliment the fashions with which they are worn.

CD JACKET COLLECTION
世界のCDジャケット・コレクション／ソフトカバー
Pages: 224 (192 in Color)　¥3,800
Featuring 700 of the world's most imaginative CD and LP covers from all musical genres, this is a must-have book for all design and music professionals.

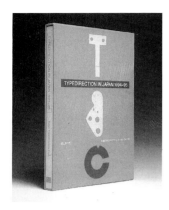

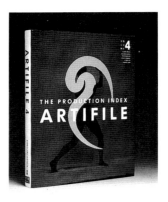

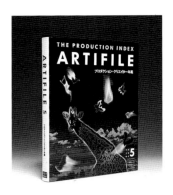

TYPO-DIRECTION IN JAPAN Vol. 6
年鑑 日本のタイポディレクション '94-'95
Pages: 250 (Full Color) ¥17,000
This book features the finest work from the international competition of graphic design in Japan. The sixth volume of our popular yearbook series is edited by the TOKYO TYPE DIRECTORS CLUB with the participation of master designers worldwide.

THE TOKYO TYPEDIRECTORS CLUB ANNUAL 1995-96
TDC 年鑑95-96
Pages: 250 (Full Color) ¥17,000
A follow-up publication to Japan's only international graphic design competition. Featuring 650 typographic artworks selected by THE TOKYO TYPEDIRECTORS CLUB, this book provides a window on the latest typographic design concepts worldwide.

The Production Index ARTIFILE Vol. 4
活躍中！広告プロダクション年鑑、第4弾
Pages: 224 (Full Color) ¥12,500
The fourth volume in our "Production Index Artifile" series features vigorously selected yearly artworks from 107 outstanding production companies and artists in Japan. An invaluable source book of the current design forefronts portraying their policies and backgrounds.

The Production Index ARTIFILE Vol.5
最新版プロダクション・クリエーター年鑑
Pages: 224(Full Color) ¥12,500
ARTIFILE 5 features artwork from a total of 100 top Japanese production companies and designers, along with company data and messages from the creators. An invaluable information source for anyone who needs to keep up with the latest developments in the graphic scene.

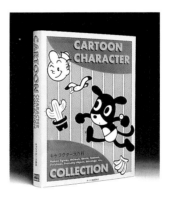

SEASONAL CAMPAIGN GRAPHICS
デパート・ショップのキャンペーン広告特集
Pages: 224 (Full Color) ¥16,000
A spirited collection of quality graphics for sales campaigns planned around the four seasons and Christmas, St. Valentines Day and the Japanese gift-giving seasons, as well as for store openings, anniversaries, and similar events.

SHOPPING BAG GRAPHICS
世界の最新ショッピング・バッグデザイン集
Pages: 224 (Full Color) ¥16,000
Over 500 samples of the latest and best of the world's shopping bag design from a wide selection of retail businesses! This volume features a selection of shopping bags originating in Tokyo, NY, LA, London, Paris, Milan and other major cities worldwide, and presented here in a useful business classification.

CARTOON CHARACTER COLLECTION
5500種のキャラクターデザイン大百科
Pages: 480 (B&W) ¥9,800
A total of 5,500 cartoons and illustrations from some of the most successful illustrations in the industry have been carefully selected for this giant, new collection. The illustrations included are classified by animals, figures, vehicles, etc, for easy reference.

カタログ・新刊のご案内について
総合カタログ、新刊案内をご希望の方は、はさみ込みのアンケートはがきを
ご返送いただくか、90円切手同封の上、ピエ・ブックス宛お申し込み下さい。

CATALOGUES ET INFORMATIONS SUR LES NOUVELLES PUBLICATIONS
Si vous désirez recevoir un exemplaire gratuit de notre catalogue général ou des détails sur nos nouvelles publications, veuillez compléter la carte réponse incluse et nous la retourner par courrierou par fax.

CATALOGS and INFORMATION ON NEW PUBLICATIONS
If you would like to receive a free copy of our general catalog or details of our new publications, please fill out the enclosed postcard and return it to us by mail or fax.

CATALOGE und INFORMATIONEN ÜBER NEUE TITLE
Wenn Sie unseren Gesamtkatalog oder Detailinformationen über unsere neuen Titel wünschen, fullen Sie bitte die beigefügte Postkarte aus und schicken Sie sie uns per Post oder Fax.

ピエ・ブックス
〒170 東京都豊島区駒込 4-14-6-301
TEL: 03-3940-8302 FAX: 03-3576-7361

P·I·E BOOKS
#301, 4-14-6, Komagome, Toshima-ku, Tokyo 170 JAPAN
TEL: 813-3940-8302 FAX: 813-3576-7361